Common Mistakes
Korean Learners Make

Common Mistakes Korean Learners Make

한국어 학습자들이 자주 하는 100가지 실수

1판 1쇄 · 1st edition published	2019. 7. 15.
1판 6쇄 · 6th edition published	2024. 6. 24.

지은이 · Written by	Talk To Me In Korean, Billy Go
책임편집 · Edited by	선경화 Kyung-hwa Sun, 대니 드루터 Dani Druther
디자인 · Designed by	선윤아 Yoona Sun, 한보람 Boram Han
녹음 · Voice Recordings by	Talk To Me In Korean
펴낸곳 · Published by	롱테일북스 Longtail Books
펴낸이 · Publisher	이수영 Su Young Lee
편집 · Copy-edited by	김보경 Florence Kim
주소 · Address	04033 서울특별시 마포구 양화로 113, 3층(서교동, 순흥빌딩)
	3rd Floor, 113 Yanghwa-ro, Mapo-gu, Seoul, KOREA
이메일 · E-mail	TTMIK@longtailbooks.co.kr
ISBN	979-11-86701-97-3

TTMIK - TALK TO ME IN KOREAN

Common Mistakes Korean Learners Make

한국어 학습자들이 자주 하는
100가지 실수

100 Ways to Sound More
Natural in Korean

Table of Contents

Preface

Mistakes. Who needs them, right? Well, I'd like to think that we all do. Mistakes are how we can learn and improve ourselves and our Korean. Nobody, no matter how smart, has learned Korean without making a mistake or two (or a thousand⋯ myself included). The downside of making mistakes is that they can sometimes be stressful, demotivating, and even embarrassing. But the upside of making mistakes outweighs the negatives – actively and regularly using the language will increase your Korean abilities exponentially more than passively and quietly trying to progress. The more you put yourself out there, the more you'll learn, and also, the faster you'll learn. Mistakes are just a part of that whole process and are unavoidable.

However, nobody really wants to make mistakes – as long as they're avoidable. We want to speak correct Korean in order to have more fluent conversations. That's where this book will come in handy. While mistakes can and will happen (often), you can prepare yourself by learning in advance what many of the most common ones are. In this way, learning the most frequently made Korean mistakes will become your armor to protect you before going into battle (figuratively, of course⋯ nobody's going to attack you if you make a mistake). You can learn from mistakes without having to make them yourself. It's almost like traveling into the future to find out what Korean mistakes you're going to make and fixing them before they happen (no time machine necessary).

I remember making countless Korean mistakes myself back when I was taking my first steps into the language in 2005; many of those mistakes were embarrassing to myself and others (and occasionally humorous). Through studying, you'll gain your own experiences and memories, and you'll be able to look back and be thankful for all of your mistakes. Good luck in your Korean studies. I'm here if and when you need me.

— Billy Go

What a pleasure working together with Billy to create this book! As someone who loves learning new languages myself, I can guarantee that this book will save you A LOT of time and embarrassment.

We have compiled 100 of the most common mistakes that Korean learners make when they either speak or write in Korean. Although it would be great if we could just understand grammar rules the first time we learn them and remember every new word we want to memorize, that is far from the reality for most people. It is only natural to make a lot of mistakes as you start expressing your own ideas in a new language, so don't be afraid to make new sentences and possibly say something incorrectly. This book will help you see what kinds of mistakes you might make in the future so you can avoid some misunderstanding or embarrassment. We hope you enjoy learning with this book!

— Hyunwoo Sun

How to use this book

⊗ THE WRONG WAY

This is a typical example of an incorrect sentence that Korean learners might often make. You can find mistakes that you often make or topics that you're unsure of in the table of contents, and then study those chapters first.

⊘ THE RIGHT WAY

This is where you'll learn the correct way to say or write the incorrect example.

WHY IS THIS WRONG?

This will briefly explain why the wrong sentence is inaccurate and how to correct it.

| CHAPTER 01 | **Korean Word Order Is Different** |

⊗ THE WRONG WAY

저는 좋아해요 한국어를 많이.
"I like Korean a lot."

⊘ THE RIGHT WAY

저는 한국어를 많이 좋아해요.
"I like Korean a lot."

WHY IS THIS WRONG?

This sentence literally translates as "I like... Korean... A lot." However, due to the words being in the wrong order, it would more likely sound like "I a lot Korean like." to a Korean.

NEVER MAKE THIS MISTAKE AGAIN

Basic Structure Korean sentence structure goes like this: subject, object, then verb. In the English sentence "Billy likes music," Billy is the subject, likes is the verb, and music is the object. In Korean, this sentence would become "Billy music likes."

빌리는 음악을 좋아해요.
"Billy likes music."

Locations Locations come before the verb. Instead of "I go to school," Korean would use "I to school go."

저는 학교에 가요.
"I go to school."

Adverbs Adverbs come directly before the verb. Instead of "I wake up early," Korean would use "I early wake up."

...rean Learners Make

 NEVER MAKE THIS MISTAKE AGAIN

Read this for more in-depth explanations and example sentences related to the mistake. You might notice some particles are written in parentheses, such as (을) in the sentence "저는 한국(을) 좋아해요." These parentheses mean that those particles are often dropped when spoken by Koreans.

MP3

Practice by listening
to a native speaker's
pronunciation,
and following along out loud.
Note that incorrect examples
are not provided.

MP3 audio files can be downloaded at
https://talktomeinkorean.com/audio.

저는 일찍 일어나요.
"I wake up early."

Adjectives Adjectives — ***descriptive verbs*** — come directly before the noun. This is
the same as in English.

예쁜 옷
"pretty clothes"

Time Time comes at either the beginning of a sentence or right after the subject.
Instead of "I swim today," Korean would use "Today I swim" or "I today swim."

오늘 저는 수영해요.
저는 오늘 수영해요.
"I swim today."

When describing the time using multiple words, organize the words in order from
largest to smallest. For example, "2:30 p.m. this afternoon" would be 오늘 오후 2시
30분, which literally means "today afternoon 2 o'clock 30 minutes."

These simple rules can be used to create longer and more complicated sentences.

저는 오늘 저녁에 재미있는 책을 천천히 읽고 싶어요.
"Tonight I want to slowly read an entertaining book."

· **BONUS EXAMPLES** ·

⊗ 저는 좋아해요 방탄소년단을 많이.
⊘ 저는 방탄소년단을 많이 좋아해요.

Meaning "I like BTS a lot."

⊗ 저는 마셔요 물을 많이.
⊘ 저는 물을 많이 마셔요.

Meaning "I drink a lot of water."

13

BONUS EXAMPLES

This includes additional examples of the mistake. You
can use these to test yourself by trying to correct the
mistakes shown and to check whether you have fully
understood the chapter.

Korean Word Order Is Different

⊗ **THE WRONG WAY**

저는 좋아해요 한국어를 많이.

"I like Korean a lot."

⊘ **THE RIGHT WAY**

저는 한국어를 많이 좋아해요.

"I like Korean a lot."

WHY IS THIS WRONG?

This sentence literally translates as "I like... Korean... A lot." However, due to the words being in the wrong order, it would more likely sound like "I a lot Korean like." to a Korean.

NEVER MAKE THIS MISTAKE AGAIN

Basic Structure Korean sentence structure goes like this: subject, object, then verb. In the English sentence "Billy likes music," **Billy** is the subject, **likes** is the verb, and **music** is the object. In Korean, this sentence would become "Billy music likes."

빌리는 음악을 좋아해요.

"Billy likes music."

Locations Locations come before the verb. Instead of "I go to school," Korean would use "I to school go."

저는 학교에 가요.

"I go to school."

Adverbs Adverbs come directly before the verb. Instead of "I wake up early," Korean would use "I early wake up."

저는 일찍 일어나요.
"I wake up early."

Adjectives Adjectives — *descriptive verbs* — come directly before the noun. This is the same as it is in English.

예쁜 옷
"pretty clothes"

Time Time comes at either the beginning of a sentence or right after the subject. Instead of "I swim today," Korean would use "Today I swim" or "I today swim."

오늘 저는 수영해요.
저는 오늘 수영해요.
"I swim today."

When describing the time using multiple words, organize the words in order from largest to smallest. For example, "2:30 p.m. this afternoon" would be 오늘 오후 2시 30분, which literally means "today afternoon 2 o'clock 30 minutes."

These simple rules can be used to create longer and more complicated sentences.

저는 오늘 저녁에 재미있는 책을 천천히 읽고 싶어요.
"Tonight I want to slowly read an entertaining book."

· · · BONUS EXAMPLES ·

⊗ 저는 좋아해요 방탄소년단을 많이.

⊘ 저는 방탄소년단을 많이 좋아해요.

> Meaning "I like BTS a lot."

⊗ 저는 마셔요 물을 많이.

⊘ 저는 물을 많이 마셔요.

> Meaning "I drink a lot of water."

To Be Or Not To Be

⊗ **THE WRONG WAY**

저는 미국에 이에요.

"I am in America."

⊘ **THE RIGHT WAY**

저는 미국에 있어요.

"I am in America."

WHY IS THIS WRONG?

Both 있다 ("to exist") and -이다 ("to be") can at times translate as "to be" in English. Using the wrong verb can easily make your sentence unintelligible in Korean. This sentence would sound like "I am (something) in America."

NEVER MAKE THIS MISTAKE AGAIN

있다 ("to exist") and -이다 ("to be") have completely different meanings in Korean, but depending on the situation, can both translate to "to be" in English. An example is the wrong sentence: "미국에 이에요." Since -이다 means "to be," 미국에 ("in America") and -이에요 ("I am") might seem to mean "I am in America."

A better way is to think of 있다 and -이다 as translating more literally. Instead, you can translate 있다 to "to exist" (as it already does) and translate -이다 as "to *equal*." Whenever the meaning of "equals" fits in a sentence, use -이다. Otherwise, use 있다.

Also, remember that -이다 has an irregular conjugation. It becomes -이에요 after a *consonant* and -예요 after a *vowel*.

저는 미국인 있어요. ⊗
"I, an American, exist."

저는 미국인이에요. ⊘
"I equal an American."

"I am American."

이것은 사과 있어요. ⊗
이것은 사과예요. ⊘
"This is an apple."

집에 강아지예요. ⊗
집에 강아지 있어요. ⊘
"There exists (is) a puppy at home."

The same difference applies to the negative forms of these verbs: 없다(↔있다) and 아니다(↔이다).

저는 미국인 없어요. ⊗
저는 미국인 아니에요. ⊘
"I am not American."

⊗ 저는 학생 있어요.

⊘ 저는 학생이에요.

Meaning   "I am a student."

⊗ 저는 선생님 없어요.

⊘ 저는 선생님 아니에요.

Meaning   "I am not a teacher."

⊗ 캐시는 지금 학교에 이에요.

⊘ 캐시는 지금 학교에 있어요.

Meaning   "Cassie is now at school."

Don't Mix Politeness Levels

⊗ **THE WRONG WAY**

나도 김치(를) 좋아해요.

"I also like kimchi."

⊘ **THE RIGHT WAY**

나도 김치(를) 좋아해.

저도 김치(를) 좋아해요.

"I also like kimchi."

WHY IS THIS WRONG?

나 is a *casual* way to say "I" or "me," while the **-아/어/여요** form (in **좋아해요**) is a *polite* ending. Speak casually, or speak politely; just don't mix different politeness levels together.

NEVER MAKE THIS MISTAKE AGAIN

나 and 저 both mean "I" or "me," but 나 is used when speaking *casually*, and 저 is used when speaking *politely* or *formally*.

The -아/어/여요 and -(스)ㅂ니다 verb endings are only used when speaking politely or formally — such as when talking with strangers or someone older — and should not be mixed with casual speech. In the same way, casual words (such as 나) should only be used with other casual verb endings.

When speaking with friends, stick to casual endings to avoid sounding awkward (and use 나). For all other situations, use non-casual endings to avoid sounding rude.

If you're not certain whether it's appropriate to use casual speech with someone or not, it's always better to be too formal than too casual. Use 저 and polite or formal speech (such as the -요 form) unless you're certain that it would be appropriate to speak casually. With close friends who are younger than you, feel free to use 나 and casual speech.

Note that 나 also appears in writing — such as in news articles or essays where the reader is unknown — together with the **plain form**, which we'll cover in a later chapter.

⊗ 나는 저스틴입니다.

✓ 나는 저스틴이야. (casual)

Meaning   "I am Justin."

✓ 저는 저스틴이에요. (polite)

✓ 저는 저스틴입니다. (formal)

⊗ 나도 갈 거예요.

✓ 나도 갈 거야. (casual)

Meaning   "I am going/coming too."

✓ 저도 갈 거예요. (polite)

✓ 저도 갈 것입니다. (formal)

⊗ 저는 한국(을) 좋아해.

✓ 나는 한국(을) 좋아해. (casual)

Meaning   "I like Korea."

✓ 저는 한국(을) 좋아해요. (polite)

✓ 저는 한국(을) 좋아합니다. (formal)

Don't Be Afraid To Be Formal

⊗ **THE WRONG WAY**

안녕하세요. 저는 경화예요.

✓ **THE RIGHT WAY**

안녕하세요. 저는 선경화입니다.

안녕하세요. 저는 선경화라고 합니다.

WHY IS THIS WRONG?

At first glance, nothing is wrong with this sentence — it's polite. However, if you were to give a speech in front of an audience, then this sentence would sound a bit too casual. Still, it's common for Korean learners to incorrectly speak this way when giving a presentation or speech.

NEVER MAKE THIS MISTAKE AGAIN

While the -(스)ㅂ니다 and -(스)ㅂ니까 verb endings are *formal* endings and are much less commonly used than the normal -요 form, they're still necessary at times. These endings are useful when giving a speech, or when you want to sound extra polite to a stranger or to anyone in a business situation.

Also, when you introduce your name formally, you should introduce your full name rather than just your first name. And if you are introducing yourself to people who don't know you, ending the sentence with -라고 합니다, which means "I am called···," sounds more natural than ending it with -입니다 ("I am···").

As -(스)ㅂ니다 and -(스)ㅂ니까 are formal endings, be careful to avoid them during any interactions with friends or close acquaintances, as they can make your sentences sound awkward (or humorous when used intentionally).

The -(스)ㅂ니다 and -(스)ㅂ니까 endings are simple to make. Just take any verb stem and attach -습니다 if it ends in a consonant (-습니까 for questions), or attach -ㅂ니다 if it ends in a vowel (-ㅂ니까 for questions). The only exception is that verb stems ending in ㄹ must have the ㄹ removed when conjugating.

먹다 → 먹습니다 or 먹습니까
하다 → 합니다 or 합니까
살다 → 삽니다 or 삽니까

Note that the following "wrong" sentences are wrong when spoken in front of people at a formal setting.

⊗ 안녕하세요, 여러분. 저는 선현우예요.

⊘ 안녕하세요, 여러분. 저는 선현우입니다.   Meaning   "Hello, everyone. I am Hyunwoo Sun."

⊘ 안녕하세요, 여러분. 저는 선현우라고 합니다.

⊗ 제 소개를 할게요.
                                         Meaning   "Let me introduce myself."
⊘ 제 소개를 하겠습니다.

⊗ 안녕하세요. 저는 현우입니다.
                                         Meaning   "Hello, I'm Hyunwoo Sun."
⊘ 안녕하세요. 저는 선현우입니다.

How Not To Form Negative Sentences

저는 일본어(를) 안 공부해요.

"I don't study Japanese."

저는 일본어를 공부하지 않아요.

저는 일본어(를) 공부 안 해요.

"I don't study Japanese."

WHY IS THIS WRONG?

One of the two ways of making a verb negative involves adding **안** to the beginning, but the rules are strict about which verbs can use this. While **하다** ("to do") can use **안**, the full verb **공부하다** ("to study") cannot.

NEVER MAKE THIS MISTAKE AGAIN

In order to make a verb negative, we need to look at whether it's an action verb (if it's about doing something) or a descriptive verb (if it's about describing something).

For action verbs that don't end with -하다, we can make them negative in two ways — either by attaching 안 to the front or -지 않다 to the verb stem.

가다 "to go" → 안 가다 "to not go" / 가지 않다 "to not go"
가르치다 "to teach" → 안 가르치다 "to not teach" / 가르치지 않다 "to not teach"

Action verbs that end with -하다 can become negative in only one way — by attaching -지 않다 to the verb stem.

공부하다 "to study" → 공부하지 않다 "to not study"
요리하다 "to cook" → 요리하지 않다 "to not cook"
운동하다 "to exercise" → 운동하지 않다 "to not exercise"

Since 하다 means "to do," any action verb ending with -하다 can therefore be thought of as meaning "to do" whatever noun comes before it. For example, you can also think of 공부하다 ("to study") as meaning "to do 공부" ("study"). This means that every such verb can be split at 하다 using the **object marker.**

공부하다 → 공부(를) 하다 "to study"
요리하다 → 요리(를) 하다 "to cook"
운동하다 → 운동(을) 하다 "to exercise"

After splitting, we can make 하다 itself negative using 안 or -지 않다.

공부(를) 안 하다
공부(를) 하지 않다
= "to not study"

요리(를) 안 하다
요리(를) 하지 않다
= "to not cook"

운동(을) 안 하다
운동(을) 하지 않다
= "to not exercise"

This only applies when what comes before -하다 is a noun. For example, 좋아하다 cannot become 좋아를 하다, 정하다 cannot become 정을 하다, and 싫어하다 cannot become 싫어를 하다.

ⓧ 오늘 안 일해요?

✓ 오늘 일 안 해요?   Meaning   "You don't work today?"

✓ 오늘 일하지 않아요?

CHAPTER 06

Special Verbs For Negative Sentences

⊗ **THE WRONG WAY**

현우 씨는 친구가 안 있어요.

"Hyunwoo doesn't have friends."

⊘ **THE RIGHT WAY**

현우 씨는 친구가 없어요.

"Hyunwoo doesn't have friends."

WHY IS THIS WRONG?

Some verbs can't use **안** to become negative, and instead have their own negative verbs that you can use. **있다** ("to exist") is one such verb that has its own negative verb - **없다** ("to not exist").

NEVER MAKE THIS MISTAKE AGAIN

Not all Korean verbs can use 안 to become negative, and a couple have their own negative verbs instead.

To say that something "does not exist," use 없다 instead of 안 있다. The same goes when using any **_descriptive verbs_** that end in -있다, such as 재미있다 ("to be entertaining," "to be fun").

재미있는 영화 "a fun movie"
재미없는 영화 "a boring (not fun) movie"

Saying 재미 안 있는 영화 ("a boring movie") would be wrong.

알다 ("to know") can become negative by using the verb 모르다 ("to not know").

Saying 안 알아요 ("I don't know.") in response to a question would also be wrong.

-이다 ("to be") can become negative by using 아니다 ("to not be"). In fact, 안 -이다 (read "아니다") is where the meaning of 아니다 originally comes from.

Also, note that while -이다 can be used after a noun, 아니다 is most often used together with the subject marker (-이 after a consonant or -가 after a vowel).

So for the sentence 좋은 생각 아니에요 ("It's not a good idea."), instead use 좋은 생각이 아니에요.

Note that this is only for 아니다, and the subject marker is not used with -이다 this way.

• • • BONUS EXAMPLES •

✕ 저는 그 책 안 있어요.

✓ 저는 그 책 없어요.

Meaning "I don't have that book."

✕ 그 영화 안 재미있어요.

✓ 그 영화 재미없어요.

Meaning "That movie is not fun."

✕ 현우 씨 전화번호 안 알아요.

✓ 현우 씨 전화번호 몰라요.

Meaning "I don't know Hyunwoo's phone number."

Honorifics Can't Be Used For Everything

⊗ **THE WRONG WAY**

여기에 강아지가 계세요.

"There is a puppy here."

⊘ **THE RIGHT WAY**

여기에 강아지가 있어요.

"There is a puppy here."

WHY IS THIS WRONG?

Honorifics shouldn't be used when talking about things or animals. Only use honorifics when talking about another person who you want to show extra respect toward. Using 계시다 (an honorific form of 있다) for an animal could be offensive when you later use that same honorific speech toward an important person.

NEVER MAKE THIS MISTAKE AGAIN

Even when you want to speak extra politely, only use honorifics when talking about someone else — not about things or animals.

사무실에 지금 사장님 계세요?

"Is the boss in the office now?"

There is an exception to this when something you're talking about is directly **owned** by someone who you want to show extra respect toward. For example, you might want to refer to your boss's "hobbies" with extra respect, although a hobby is a thing. When used in this way, the honorifics are not showing respect to the thing, but to the person who the thing belongs to. However, in this case the honorific form of 있다 becomes 있으시다, not 계시다. This is because 계시다 can only be used to show extra respect to a person.

우산 계세요? ⊗
우산 있으세요? ⊘
"Do you have an umbrella?"

고민 계세요? ⊗
고민 있으세요? ⊘
"Do you have any concerns?"

· · · BONUS EXAMPLES ·

⊗　강아지가 아프세요.

⊘　강아지가 아파요.

Meaning　"(My) puppy is sick."

⊗　아메리카노 나오셨습니다.

⊘　아메리카노 나왔습니다.

Meaning　"The Americano is ready."

⊗　옷이 예쁘세요.

⊘　옷이 예뻐요.

Meaning　"I like your clothes."

Be Humble When Talking About Yourself

⊗ **THE WRONG WAY**

선생님, 도와줄게요.

"Teacher, I'll help you."

⊘ **THE RIGHT WAY**

선생님, 도와 드릴게요.

"Teacher, I'll help you."

WHY IS THIS WRONG?

Humble verbs work by making your sentence sound like you're lowering (or humbling) yourself down to someone who is *higher* than you to show extra respect. And not using humble verbs when you should be can leave a sentence sounding impolite.

NEVER MAKE THIS MISTAKE AGAIN

Unlike honorific verbs, humble verbs are used when talking about *yourself* — not someone else. Luckily, there are not many humble verbs to learn. Let's look at two — 드리다 and 뵈다.

드리다 This takes the place of 주다 ("to give") when *you* (or the subject of the sentence) are giving someone something — someone who you want to show extra respect toward.

저는 할머니께 용돈을 드리고 싶어요.

"I want to give my grandmother some spending money."

드리다 also takes the place of 주다 when used at the end of other verbs. This is common when you are doing something for someone who you want to show extra respect toward. 도와주다 can become 도와 드리다, 해 주다 can become 해 드리다, and so forth.

저는 정말 그렇게 해 드리고 싶어요.
"I really want to do it for you."

뵈다 This takes the place of 보다 ("to see") when **you** (or the subject of the sentence) are the one who will be seeing someone who you want to show extra respect toward.

내일 뵐게요!
"I'll see you tomorrow!"

· · · **BONUS EXAMPLES** ·

⊗ 이따 볼게요.

✓ 이따 뵐게요. (polite)   Meaning   "I'll see you later."

✓ 이따 뵙겠습니다. (formal)

⊗ 마실 것 좀 줄까요?   "Would you like something
                                  Meaning   to drink?"
✓ 마실 것 좀 드릴까요?

⊗ 제가 부모님을 도와줬어요.   "I helped out my parents."
                                  Meaning
✓ 제가 부모님을 도와 드렸어요.

Don't Say "You"

⊗ **THE WRONG WAY**

너는 이제 가도 돼요.

"You can go now."

⊘ **THE RIGHT WAY**

이제 가도 돼요.

"You can go now."

WHY IS THIS WRONG?

Most of the time, it's unnecessary to say "you." Using 너, 당신, and other words for "you" can often sound awkward and even rude.

NEVER MAKE THIS MISTAKE AGAIN

Only use words for "you" when appropriate. Here's an overview of those words:

너 Only use this with close friends who are younger than you. With others, it sounds very rude.

당신 Only use this in these specific situations:

A. When you are addressing your spouse (commonly used among middle-aged or older people).

B. When you have to or want to say "you" in an honorific or romantic way in writing.

C. When you are angry at someone and don't mind fighting or arguing with that person.

D. When you are talking about someone (who is not present) in an honorific way — in this case, 당신 will translate as "he/his/him" or "she/her."

The most common way Koreans say "you" is by not saying "you" at all. Instead of these two words, Koreans will use a person's **name** or **title**.

When using a **_friend's_** name, also add -이 to the end of their name if it ends in a consonant. For other **_acquaintances_**, use 씨.

Friend: 민우 or 석진**이**
Acquaintance: 민우 씨 or 석진 **씨**.

For anyone older than you or anyone who you need to show respect to, use their title. Titles include everything from 누나, 형, 언니, 오빠 (for friends) to 사장님 (for a boss) and 선생님 (for a teacher).

In addition, when asking a question to someone, it can be assumed that you mean "you," so saying "you" is often unnecessary.

BONUS EXAMPLES

(x) 너는 먼저 먹어도 돼요.

(✓) 먼저 먹어도 돼요.

> Meaning "You can eat first."

(x) 너는 언제 갈 거예요?

(✓) 언제 갈 거예요?

> Meaning "When are you going to go/leave?"

(x) 당신은 게임(을) 좋아해요?

(✓) 게임(을) 좋아해요?

> Meaning "Do you like games?"

There Is No "He" Or "She"

⊗ **THE WRONG WAY**

그녀는 한국 사람이에요.

"She's a Korean."

⊘ **THE RIGHT WAY**

그 사람 한국 사람이에요.

"She's a Korean."

WHY IS THIS WRONG?

그 and 그녀 are used when Koreans directly translate the English words "he" and "she" into Korean writing, such as in textbook example sentences. These words sound awkward if used in speech.

NEVER MAKE THIS MISTAKE AGAIN

To say "he" or "she" or just "that person," use 그 사람, which literally means "that person." If you are referring to a person who is close to you, you could say 이 사람 ("this person"), and to a person who is away from both you and the listener but who is still visible, you could say 저 사람 ("that person over there"). If you want or need to specify the gender, you can use 남자 for a man and 여자 for a woman, such as 그 여자, 저 남자, etc.

저 사람 한국 사람이에요.

"That person over there is a Korean."

저 남자 한국 사람이에요.

"That man over there is a Korean."

If "he" or "she" is a person whom you and the listener both have to use honorifics to, you should use 그분 ("that person"), 이분 ("this person"), and 저분 ("that person over there") instead of 그 사람, 이 사람, and 저 사람. If you want to or need to specify the gender, you can also use 남자 or 여자, such as 그 여자분, 저 남자분, etc.

저 여자분은 누구세요?
"Who is that woman over there?"

If you know the person's name or title, you can use it instead.

경은 씨 한국 사람이에요.
"Kyeong-eun is a Korean."

Also, in many situations, you can simply omit the subject. For example, if you say 한국 사람이에요 about someone while already talking about them, the listener will simply know that you are referring to him or her even without saying the words for "he" or "she."

If you are referring to a person whom you would use casual language to (반말), you can use 걔 ("that person"). 걔 originally comes from a contraction of 그 아이 ("that kid").

걔 한국 사람이에요.

You can also use 얘 ("this person"), which comes from a contraction of 이 아이, meaning "this kid." Or if a person is away from both you and the listener but is still visible, you could use 쟤 ("that person over there"), which comes from a contraction of 저 아이, meaning "that kid over there." Again, if you want to or need to specify the gender, you can attach 남자 or 여자, such as 그 남자아이 (or 그 남자애) and 이 여자 아이 (or 이 여자애).

· · · **BONUS EXAMPLES** ·

⊗ 그는 제 동생이에요.

　　　　　　　　　　　　　Meaning　　"He is my younger brother."

⊘ 이/그/저 사람은 제 동생이에요.

Please Don't Say "Please"

⊗ **THE WRONG WAY**

부산역 주세요.

"Busan Station, please."

✓ **THE RIGHT WAY**

부산역(으로) 가 주세요.

"Please go to Busan Station."

WHY IS THIS WRONG?

If you were to say this to a taxi driver, it would sound like you were asking them to **give** you Busan Station. This is because 주세요 literally means "Please give me."

NEVER MAKE THIS MISTAKE AGAIN

Although 주세요 is a common translation of "please" in many contexts, it can't always be used the same way that you use "please" in English because 주세요 is only a polite way of asking someone to give you something. Only use it when you want to say "Please give me."

메뉴판 주세요.

"Please give me a menu."

물 더 주세요.

"Please give me more water."

To ask for someone to "please" do something, you can attach 주세요 to the end of a conjugated verb. To do this, conjugate a verb and attach -(으)세요 or -아/어/여 주세요. If you use -(으)세요, it simply means "Please do it," and is just a polite or soft-sounding way of ordering or commanding someone to do something. On the other hand, if you use -아/어/여 주세요, it can sound like you are requesting someone to do something for you, like asking "Please do it (for me)."

숙제하세요.

"Please do your homework."

제 숙제를 해 주세요.

"Please do my homework (for me)."

앉으세요.

"Please take a seat."

앉아 주세요.

"Please take a seat (for my benefit)."

저를 믿어 주세요.

"Please believe me."

저랑 같이 가 주세요.

"Please go together with me."

If you really need to say "please" by itself, you can use 제발 ("please"). Note that 제발 sounds dramatic — like you are begging someone — and is much less common.

제발 가지 마!

"Please, don't go!"

제발 제 말 좀 들어 주세요.

"Please, listen to what I'm saying."

···· **BONUS EXAMPLES** ·········

  ⊗   잠깐/잠시 주세요.

  ⊘   잠깐/잠시 기다려 주세요.

Meaning   "One moment, please."

Counting Heads

파티에 일 명이 왔어요.

"One person came to the party."

파티에 한 명이 왔어요.

"One person came to the party."

WHY IS THIS WRONG?

일 means "one," but it cannot be used with the *counter* 명 for counting people.

NEVER MAKE THIS MISTAKE AGAIN

There are two number systems in Korean — pure Korean numbers and Sino-Korean numbers. The number system you will use depends on what it is you are counting. Here's a quick overview of the pure Korean numbers 1 to 10:

Pure Korean numbers: 하나, 둘, 셋, 넷, 다섯, 여섯, 일곱, 여덟, 아홉, 열

To count people, use pure Korean numbers together with the *counter* 명. To say "five people," it would be 다섯 명. "Ten people" would be 열 명. And "one person" is 한 명 — not 하나 명. Let's talk about why.

한, 두, 세, 네, 스무

The numbers 1 to 4, and 20 change whenever they're used in front of a *counter* (such as 명). All other numbers will remain the same, so while "20 people" is 스무 명, "21 people" is 스물 한 명, and so on.

Also, when you are counting a relatively small number of people, like five people or up to a couple dozen people, you can also use the counter 사람 instead of 명. But for that as well, you can't use the Sino-Korean numbers.

여기에 오 사람 있어요. ⊗
여기에 다섯 사람 있어요. ⊘
여기에 다섯 명 있어요. ⊘
"There are five people here."

• • • **BONUS EXAMPLES** •

⊗ 사 명이에요.

⊘ 네 명이에요.

> Meaning

"There are four people."

⊗ 일 반에 십오 명의 학생이 있어요.

⊘ 한 반에 열다섯 명의 학생이 있어요.

> Meaning

"There are fifteen students in one class."

⊗ 아직 이 명 안 왔어요.

⊘ 아직 두 명 안 왔어요.

> Meaning

"Two people haven't come yet."

CHAPTER 13

Counting Things

⊗ THE WRONG WAY

컵 둘 사고 싶어요.

"I want to buy two cups."

⊘ THE RIGHT WAY

컵 두 개 사고 싶어요.

"I want to buy two cups."

WHY IS THIS WRONG?

When counting objects, you must use a **counter**. Which counter you use will depend on what you're counting. Not using a counter can make the sentence sound unnatural and incomplete.

NEVER MAKE THIS MISTAKE AGAIN

Everything that can be counted has an appropriate counter to use. When counting people, you used 명, and when counting objects, you can use 개.

개 This counter is used for **things in general** which don't already have their own counter. Although this is a general use counter for everything, it should not be used when there is a better counter available. It's used together with pure Korean numbers. Remember that the numbers 1 to 4 and 20 will change when used directly before a counter.

의자 다섯 개
"five chairs"

공 세 개
"three balls"

상자 열 개
"10 boxes"

Notice how what you're counting comes first, followed by the number, and then the counter. This is the same for all counters whenever you're specifying what you're counting. Also, remember that if it's already clear what you're counting (for example, "How many cups did you buy?"), then it would be unnecessary and repetitive to say it again.

컵 아홉 개 샀어요. ⊗
아홉 개 샀어요. ⊘
"I bought nine (cups)."

어제 모니터 열 개 샀어요.
"I bought 10 monitors yesterday."

저는 의자 세 개 있어요.
"I have three chairs."

There is an exception for the number one (하나) when used with this counter. It's alright to simply use 하나 without this counter when you want to emphasize that it's only one.

핸드폰을 한 개 사고 싶어요.
핸드폰을 하나 사고 싶어요.
"I want to buy one mobile phone."

There are many other counters — for counting everything from bottles (병), paper (장), and books (권) to large appliances (대) and more. If you're completely unable to remember which specific counter to use in other situations, at least use 개 to clarify you mean "thing" and to prevent the sentence from becoming too awkward.

···· **BONUS EXAMPLES** ···

⊗ 셋 선물 있어요.

⊘ 선물 세 개 있어요.

Meaning   "I have three presents."

That's Not The Only Way To Say "Only"

저는 친구가 한 명만 있어요.

"I have only one friend."

저는 친구가 한 명밖에 없어요.

"I only have one friend."

WHY IS THIS WRONG?

This sentence grammatically makes sense, but sounds stiff and unnatural. **한 명만** means "only one person," but -**만** is only used in a few specific situations.

NEVER MAKE THIS MISTAKE AGAIN

Instead of -만, attach -밖에 after a noun followed by any *negative verb* (e.g. 없다, 모르다, 안 가다, etc.). -밖에 literally means "outside of" or "other than," and when used with a negative verb, it means "nothing outside of" — therefore translating naturally as "only."

In our example, we can change 한 명만 to 한 명밖에, and 있다 ("to exist") to its negative verb 없다 ("to not exist"). Using -밖에 sounds more natural and better emphasizes the meaning of something *lacking* — in this case, that there is only one friend and not more. Here are some more examples:

사과를 세 개밖에 안 먹었어요.

"I only ate three apples."

저는 영어밖에 할 줄 몰라요.

"I only know how to speak English."

-만 is still used in two situations. In these two situations, -밖에 *cannot* be used.

First, -만 is used when telling someone to do something. These are called *imperative sentences*.

하나만 고르세요.
"Please choose only one."

Second, -만 is used in sentences with "if." These are called *conditional sentences*.

이것만 하면 끝나요.
"If I only do this, I'll be done."

-만 can also be used in any situation (even the incorrect example), but only when you don't need to express that something is *lacking*.

저는 주말에 운동만 해요.
"I only work out on the weekend."

In this sentence, you could say 저는 주말에 운동밖에 안 해요 if you want to emphasize that the only thing you do is work out on the weekend and that something is insufficient or lacking because of that (perhaps you wish you could do other things). However, because it uses -만, it is not expressing that something is lacking, meaning that there's nothing to complain about here.

· · · BONUS EXAMPLES ·

⊗ 지갑에 돈이 천 원만 있어요.

✓ 지갑에 돈이 천 원밖에 없어요.

Meaning   "I only have 1,000 won in my wallet."

⊗ 석진 씨는 축구만 알아요.

✓ 석진 씨는 축구밖에 몰라요.

Meaning   "Seokjin only knows about soccer."

How To Raise A Pet

⊗ **THE WRONG WAY**

저는 고양이를 가지고 있어요.

"I have a cat."

⊘ **THE RIGHT WAY**

저는 고양이를 키우고 있어요.

"I have a cat."

WHY IS THIS WRONG?

가지다 and **가지고 있다** mean "to have," so grammatically, this sentence means "I have a cat" and makes sense. However, Koreans don't say **가지다** or **가지고 있다** about living things in most contexts because **가지다** can only be applied to something you "own" or "possess."

NEVER MAKE THIS MISTAKE AGAIN

To say that you have something, you can use either 있다 ("to exist") or the verb 가지다 ("to have," "to carry").

저는 핸드폰이 있어요.
저는 핸드폰을 가지고 있어요.
"I have a cell phone."

Using 가지다 has a stronger meaning stating that you actually own something and might be carrying it on you. However, don't use 가지다 when talking about your pets. Instead, use the verb 키우다 ("to raise").

저는 개를 가지고 싶어요. ⊗
저는 개를 키우고 싶어요. ⊘
"I want to have a dog (as a pet)."

저는 개 한 마리 키워요.
"I have a dog."

저희 집은 고양이 안 키워요.
"We don't have a cat at our house."

And you can also conjugate the verb 키우다 to 키우고 있어요, which literally means that you are "currently raising a pet."

저는 개 한 마리 키우고 있어요.
"I have a dog."

저는 개 열 마리 키우고 있어요.
"I have ten dogs."

· · · BONUS EXAMPLES ·

⊗ 집에서 (반려)동물 가지고 있어요?

⊘ 집에서 (반려)동물 키우고 있어요?   Meaning   "Do you have a pet in
your house?"

⊘ 집에서 (반려)동물 키워요?

⊗ 가지고 있는 (반려)동물 있어요?

⊘ 키우고 있는 (반려)동물 있어요?   Meaning   "Do you have a pet?"

⊘ 키우는 (반려)동물 있어요?

⊗ 동생 가지고 있어요?   "Do you have a younger
Meaning   sibling?"
⊘ 동생 있어요?

Counting Animals

⊗ **THE WRONG WAY**

동물원에 강아지 두 개 있어요.

"There are two dogs in the zoo."

✓ **THE RIGHT WAY**

동물원에 강아지 두 마리 있어요.

"There are two dogs in the zoo."

WHY IS THIS WRONG?

The **counter 개** can only be used to count objects — not people or animals. Using the wrong counter can sound disrespectful (such as counting a person with the animal counter) or just plain awkward (such as in this example).

NEVER MAKE THIS MISTAKE AGAIN

As we learned previously, we can count people with 명, a person's age with 살, and general things with 개. There are counters for counting everything imaginable, but several of the most commonly used ones are also the ones most commonly misused.

마리 This counter is used for **animals**. It's used together with pure Korean numbers. Remember that the numbers 1 to 4 and 20 will change when used directly before a counter. Be careful to not use the counter 명 ("people") when counting animals, as it can sound like the animal you're counting is a human.

거북이 네 마리
"four turtles"

코끼리 한 마리
"one elephant"

두더지 스무 마리
"twenty moles"

닭 두 마리를 키우고 있어요.
"I have two chickens."

오늘 곰 다섯 마리 봤어요.
"I saw five bears today."

⋯ BONUS EXAMPLES ⋯

ⓧ 고양이 몇 개 키워요?

✓ 고양이 몇 마리 키워요?

Meaning "How many cats do you have?"

ⓧ 닭 한 개가 사라졌어요.

✓ 닭 한 마리가 사라졌어요.

Meaning "One of the chickens is gone."

ⓧ 집 앞에서 고양이 한 개 봤어요.

✓ 집 앞에서 고양이 한 마리 봤어요.

Meaning "I saw a cat in front of the house."

CHAPTER 17

Just Because You Don't, Doesn't Mean You Can't

⊗ **THE WRONG WAY**

저는 한국말을 잘 안 해요.

"I don't speak Korean well."

⊘ **THE RIGHT WAY**

저는 한국말을 잘 못해요.

"I can't speak Korean well."

WHY IS THIS WRONG?

잘 안 해요 literally means "doesn't (do) well," but 안 해요 ("doesn't do") has a different meaning from "can't." What this sentence actually means is that you might or might not speak Korean, but that you simply choose *not to* speak Korean well. Or since 잘 can also have the meaning of "often," it could even mean "I don't speak Korean often."

NEVER MAKE THIS MISTAKE AGAIN

The reason for this mistake comes from thinking in English. This problem occurs most frequently in the *present tense*. "Don't" can be used in English to mean both "does not (by choice)" and "cannot." However, in Korean, these will use separate words.

We can use 안 and the ending -지 않다 to make a verb negative (depending on the type of verb), and when used with an *action verb*, these forms imply that you're not doing something by your own choice. These forms also do not carry the meaning of "can't."

한국어를 공부 안 해요.
한국어를 공부하지 않아요.
"I don't study Korean (by choice)."

Using this form to say that you "don't" speak Korean also means that you're not doing so by of your own choice — whether you actually can or can't speak it.

To say "can't," you can use 못 (in the same way and situations as 안) or the ending -지 못하다.

안 잊을게요.
잊지 않을게요.
"I won't forget."

못 잊어요.
잊지 못해요.
"I can't forget."

매운 음식을 안 먹어요.
매운 음식을 먹지 않아요.
"I don't eat spicy food (by choice)."

매운 음식을 못 먹어요.
매운 음식을 먹지 못해요.
"I can't eat spicy food."

안 도와줄 거예요.
도와주지 않을 거예요.
"I won't help you (by choice)."

못 도와줘요.
도와주지 못해요.
"I can't help you (even if I wanted to)."

Note that if the verb is 잘하다 ("to do something well, to be good at something"), it doesn't become 못 잘하다. Instead, it becomes 잘 못하다, meaning "to be not good at something" or "can't do something well."

저는 요리를 잘 못해요.
저는 요리를 잘하지 못해요.
"I can't cook well."

Listing Past Tense Actions

⊗ **THE WRONG WAY**

저는 어제 밥 먹었고 집에 갔어요.

"Yesterday, I ate and then went home."

⊘ **THE RIGHT WAY**

저는 어제 밥 먹고 집에 갔어요.

"Yesterday, I ate and then went home."

WHY IS THIS WRONG?

Grammatically, this sentence is acceptable, but it sounds a bit repetitive and awkward. When speaking in the past tense, only the final verb in a sentence needs to be conjugated to past tense.

NEVER MAKE THIS MISTAKE AGAIN

When using past tense, it's not necessary to conjugate every single verb in the sentence to past tense. Only the final verb needs to be conjugated in order to sound natural. Conjugating every verb is grammatically acceptable, but it can be repetitive and unnecessary.

숙제(를) 다 했고 친구(를) 만났어요. ⊗
숙제(를) 다 하고 친구(를) 만났어요. ⊘
"I did all of the homework and then met a friend."

This applies not only to connecting sentences with the -고 ending, but also with the -아/어/여서 ending. However, when using the -아/어/여서 ending, it is not only repetitive and awkward to conjugate every verb to past tense, but it's also grammatically incorrect.

배가 고팠어서 점심을 일찍 먹었어요. ⊗
배가 고파서 점심을 일찍 먹었어요. ⊘
"I was hungry, so I ate lunch early."

When the two actions listed in one sentence are not related to each other, however, it is acceptable to conjugate both verbs.

서울에는 비가 안 왔고 부산에는 비가 왔어요. ⊘
서울에는 비가 안 오고 부산에는 비가 왔어요. ⊘
"It didn't rain in Seoul, and it rained in Busan."

| ⊗ | 어제 영화 봤고 볼링 쳤어요. | Meaning | "Yesterday, we saw a movie and went bowling." |
| ⊘ | 어제 영화 보고 볼링 쳤어요. | | |

| ⊗ | 뉴스 봤고 잤어요. | Meaning | "I watched the news and went to bed." |
| ⊘ | 뉴스 보고 잤어요. | | |

| ⊗ | 아팠어서 회사에 못 갔어요. | Meaning | "I was ill, so I couldn't go to work." |
| ⊘ | 아파서 회사에 못 갔어요. | | |

Not Using "And" Enough

⊗ THE WRONG WAY

오늘은 김치, 밥, 햄버거(를) 먹었어요.

"Today I ate kimchi, rice, a hamburger."

✓ THE RIGHT WAY

오늘은 김치하고 밥하고 햄버거(를) 먹었어요.
오늘은 김치랑 밥이랑 햄버거(를) 먹었어요.

"Today I ate kimchi and rice and a hamburger."

WHY IS THIS WRONG?

This sentence grammatically makes sense, but sounds stiff and unnatural when spoken. Koreans almost always use a particle between nouns when listing things in speech. Therefore, this sentence would sound like you were reading a written sentence.

NEVER MAKE THIS MISTAKE AGAIN

There are three ways of connecting nouns in Korean:

-과/와 This is the most formal and standard way to say "and." Attach -과 if the noun ends in a **consonant**, or attach -와 if it ends in a **vowel**.

햄과 양파와 밥
"ham and onions and rice"

-하고 This is less formal, but fine for conversational usage. Attach -하고 directly after the noun.

햄하고 양파하고 밥
"ham and onions and rice"

-(이)랑 This is the least formal way, and is mainly only used in casual speech. Attach -이랑 if the noun ends in a **consonant**, or attach -랑 if it ends in a **vowel**.

햄이랑 양파랑 밥
"ham and onions and rice"

Whichever of these three you choose, stick with one — don't mix them.

All three of these can also be used to mean "with."

제 친구와 공원에서 놀았어요.
"I played at the park with my friend."

엄마랑 영화 보러 갔어요.
"I went to see a movie with my mom."

One more way to say "and" is **그리고**. However, 그리고 is not often used to connect nouns together, especially in spoken language. Instead, 그리고 is used at the start of a sentence or phrase to mean "and," "and then," or "and also."

그리고 케이크랑 피자 샀어요.
"I bought cake and pizza."

· · BONUS EXAMPLES · · · · ·

Written/Formal	Spoken/Casual	Meaning
양파와 당근을 넣으세요.	양파랑 당근을 넣으세요. 양파하고 당근을 넣으세요.	"Add the onion and carrot."
화장지와 세제, 그리고 샴푸를 사야 돼요.	화장지랑 세제랑 샴푸(를) 사야 돼요.	"I need to buy toilet paper, detergent, and shampoo."

CHAPTER 20

When To Use "If" And "When"

⊗ **THE WRONG WAY**

우리가 만날 때 재미있을 거예요.

"It'll be fun when we meet."

⊘ **THE RIGHT WAY**

우리가 만나면 재미있을 거예요.

"It'll be fun when we meet."

WHY IS THIS WRONG?

The grammar forms used to say "if" and "when" can sometimes be similar when translated in English, but they have different meanings. This sentence would mean that it'll be fun at the exact time when you meet, and perhaps not after that, when you're talking and spending time together.

NEVER MAKE THIS MISTAKE AGAIN

Verb Stem + -(으)면

To say "if" and "when," attach -으면 to the verb stem after a **consonant**, or attach -면 after a **vowel**. Verb stems ending in ㄹ, ㅂ, or ㅎ will drop those letters first. In addition, verb stems ending in ㅂ will attach 우 before -면 (becoming -우면 after the verb stem).

This form is used for hypothetical situations — "if" or "when" something happens. It does not mean that something will happen for sure, but only that it might, and is used to talk about "if" or "when" it does. For example, 공부하면 could mean either "If you study..." or "When you study..." You can also think of it meaning "Hypothetically, let's say that you study."

Verb Stem + -(으)ㄹ 때

To say "when" (and not "if"), attach -을 때 to the verb stem after a **consonant**, or attach -ㄹ 때 after a **vowel**.

This form is used to talk about the very moment or time that something happens. For example, 공부할 때 could mean "When you study…" or "At the moment or time that you study…" Because of this, the example sentence would be incorrect because it's only talking about the moment when these two people meet (만날 때).

However, there are many times when either form can be used. Just understand that, although a sentence might grammatically make sense, its meaning could be different from what you were trying to say.

시간 있을 때 밥 먹자.
"Let's eat when (at the moment) you have time."

시간 있으면 밥 먹자.
"Let's eat when (or if) you have time."

집에 갈 때…
"When (at the moment) I go home…"

집에 가면…
"When (or if) I go home…"

· · · BONUS EXAMPLES ·

ⓧ 집에 도착할 때 문자 해요.

✓ 집에 도착하면 문자 해요.

> Meaning

"Text me when you get home."

ⓧ 석진 씨 도착할 때 저한테 알려 주세요.

✓ 석진 씨 도착하면 저한테 알려 주세요.

> Meaning

"Please let me know when Seokjin arrives."

WHAT'S WRONG WITH THIS SENTENCE?

선글라스를 입고 싶어요.

✓ See Chapter 26

CHAPTER 21

Plural Forms Are More Flexible In Korean

⊗ **THE WRONG WAY**

세 가지 음식들을 먹어 봤어요.

"I tried three types of foods."

⊘ **THE RIGHT WAY**

세 가지 음식을 먹어 봤어요.

"I tried three types of foods."

WHY IS THIS WRONG?

Plural nouns are often not necessary in Korean if a noun is accompanied by a counting unit or words that indicate how many of something there are.

NEVER MAKE THIS MISTAKE AGAIN

Plural nouns can be made by attaching -들 to the end. 고양이 ("cat") can become 고양이들 ("cats"), and 사람 ("person") can become 사람들 ("people").

In Korean, it can be assumed that any noun is singular or plural just by looking at the context. In most cases, it's not necessary to turn a noun into a plural using -들.

고양이 두 마리를 봤어요.

"I saw two cats."

In this sentence, 고양이 must translate to "cats" and not just "cat" because there are two of them. In addition, Koreans would never say 고양이들 두 마리를 봤어요 or 고양이 두 마리들을 봤어요.

동물원에서 코끼리를 봤어요.

"I saw an elephant at the zoo."

"I saw elephants at the zoo."

Here as well, unless it's absolutely important to say there were multiple elephants, adding -들 is unnecessary. It can probably be assumed you saw more than one since you were at a zoo.

왜 이렇게 신발들이 많아요? **(less natural)**
왜 이렇게 신발이 많아요? **(more natural)**
"Why are there so many shoes?"

So, when is -들 even used?

When there are no other words that would indicate that the noun is plural in a sentence (such as 세 가지, 두 마리, 많다, etc.), and when it would be possible for listeners or readers to misunderstand it as a singular noun, attach -들.

인기 있는 스마트폰이 여기 있어요.
Here is a popular smartphone.

인기 있는 스마트폰들이 여기 있어요.
Here are popular smartphones.

Also, it's natural to use -들 when talking about a noun *in general* — without knowing how many there are. In fact, if you add the phrase "in general" after your noun when translating it to English, and if it sounds better, then you can attach -들.

한국 사람은 이렇게 생각해요.
"A Korean thinks like this."
"Koreans think like this."

한국 사람들은 이렇게 생각해요.
"Koreans (in general) think like this."

How Are You?

⊗ **THE WRONG WAY**

잘 지냈어요?

"How are you?"

⊘ **THE RIGHT WAY**

안녕하세요!

"Hello!"

WHY IS THIS WRONG?

Asking **잘 지냈어요** to someone who you just saw yesterday (or very recently) sounds awkward, as it seems like you haven't seen them in a while.

NEVER MAKE THIS MISTAKE AGAIN

잘 지내다 ("to be well" or "to get along well") is used to ask how a person is doing, or how a person is getting along with someone. However, a much better translation for 잘 지냈어요 than "How are you doing?" would be "How have you been?"

In addition, using 잘 지내다 in any conjugation is best for when asking how someone is doing if you don't already know — unlike in English, where it's normal to ask someone "How are you?" even if you've just seen them yesterday. In Korean, this expression is only used when enough time has passed for you to no longer know how a person is doing or getting along with someone, or at least after a couple of days.

Instead of asking 잘 지냈어요, 잘 지내요, or 잘 지내세요 when not much time has passed since your last meeting, consider saying 안녕하세요 ("Hello.") or simply 안녕 to a close friend.

Alternatively, you can ask them if they've eaten yet using 밥(을) 먹다 ("to eat a meal"), which is a common greeting in Korea.

밥 먹었어(요)?
식사하셨어요? (honorific speech)
"Did you eat?"

To someone who you just saw yesterday:

ⓧ 잘 있었어요?

ⓥ 안녕하세요!

Meaning   "How are you?"

ⓧ 잘 지내요?

ⓥ 안녕하세요!

Meaning   "How are you?"

ⓧ 잘 지내?

ⓥ 안녕!

Meaning   "How are you?"

Let's Not Do It

<table>
<tr><td>

(×) **THE WRONG WAY**

사장님, 회의하러 갑시다!

"Boss, let's go have a meeting!"

</td><td>

(✓) **THE RIGHT WAY**

사장님, 회의하러 가실까요?

사장님, 회의하러 가시겠어요?

사장님, 회의하러 가시겠습니까?

"Boss, shall we go have a meeting?"

</td></tr>
</table>

WHY IS THIS WRONG?

The form used to say "let's" in the example is only used when talking down to someone else. This form should not be used in formal situations, and can also sound awkward when used with friends.

NEVER MAKE THIS MISTAKE AGAIN

There are several ways to say "let's" in Korean. Overall, saying "let's" is *suggesting* to someone else to do something with you.

-(으)ㅂ시다 Even though this form has the honorific suffix -시-, it is only used when talking down to someone from a higher position (such as a boss to their employees) or to someone close to you whom you cannot use casual speech toward (such as an adult son to his mother). As such, it's neither polite, nor casual, and it should therefore be avoided. To use this form, take a verb stem and attach -읍시다 if it ends in a *consonant*, or attach -ㅂ시다 if it ends in a *vowel*.

퇴근합시다!
"Let's finish work!"

-자 This form is only used in *casual speech*. To use this form, take a verb stem and attach -자.

밥 먹자!
"Let's eat!"

같이 + -요 This form is acceptable to use in most situations outside of formal speech. To use this form, add the adverb 같이 ("together") before a verb conjugated to the -요 form. With close friends, you can remove the -요.

저랑 같이 운동해요.
"Let's exercise together."

-(으)ㄹ까(요)? This form does not mean "let's," but instead, is a polite way to suggest "shall we" do something or to ask "could something be" a certain way. To use this form, take a verb stem and attach -을까(요)? after a **consonant**, or attach -ㄹ까(요)? after a **vowel**. The -요 can be removed for casual speech. If you are talking to someone older or to someone in a higher position than yourself, you should attach -시- and say (같이) -(으)실까요?

이쪽으로 (같이) 가실까요?
"Shall we go this way (together)?"

-(으)시겠어요? This form does not mean "let's" either, but instead, is a polite and formal way to ask about someone's intentions. A literal translation of this form could be "Would you care to + verb, sir/ma'am?" To use this form, take a verb stem and attach -으시겠어요? if it ends in a **consonant**, or attach -시겠어요? if it ends in a **vowel**. If you add -습니까? Instead of -어요?, it sounds even more formal.

식사하시겠어요?
식사하시겠습니까?
"Would you care to have breakfast/lunch/dinner?"

CHAPTER 24

How Much Later Will It Be?

⊗ **THE WRONG WAY**

A: **2시간 뒤에 만나자.**

"Let's meet in two hours."

B: **그래. 나중에 보자!**

"Ok. See you later!"

⊘ **THE RIGHT WAY**

A: **2시간 뒤에 만나자.**

"Let's meet in two hours."

B: **그래. 이따 보자!**

"Ok. See you in a bit!"

WHY IS THIS WRONG?

나중에 means "later" as in "much later." In the example, saying **나중에 보자** could cause the other person to feel sad because you would be replying that you want to see them much later instead of only two hours later.

NEVER MAKE THIS MISTAKE AGAIN

Both 나중에 and 이따(가) mean "later," but are used in different situations.

나중에 This means "later," often in the sense of "not today, but *later*." In this way, you can think of it as meaning "much later."

나중에 다시 오세요.

"Please come back later (but not today)."

이따(가) This means "later," in the sense of "within today, after a *short* time." The 가 at the end is optional, and adding or removing it does not change the meaning.

이따가 다시 오세요.

"Please come back a bit later (and before the end of today)."

One more thing to mention is 있다가, which has the same pronunciation as 이따가 but a different meaning and usage. 이따가 is commonly misspelled as 있다가, but these are two separate concepts. 있다가 comes from 있다 ("to exist," or here meaning "to stay") and the -다가 form, which is used to show that something is happening right when something else happens.

10분만 더 있다가 나가자.
"Let's leave after (staying) just 10 more minutes."

나중에	이따가
나중에 전화할게요. "I will call you later (but not today)."	이따(가) 전화할게요. "I will call you later today."
나중에 주세요. "Please give it to me later (but not today)."	이따(가) 주세요. "Please give it to me later today."
나중에 할까요? "Shall we do it later (but not today)?"	이따(가) 할까요? "Shall we do it later today?"

Hot Weather That'll Burn Your Finger

⊗ **THE WRONG WAY**

어제 날씨가 차가웠어요.

"Yesterday's weather was cold."

⊘ **THE RIGHT WAY**

어제 날씨가 추웠어요.

"Yesterday's weather was cold."

WHY IS THIS WRONG?

차갑다 is usually used to describe things that are cold to the touch, but not the weather. This sentence would be like saying the weather is so cold that it could freeze your finger.

NEVER MAKE THIS MISTAKE AGAIN

There are two words for each "hot" and "cold" that you'll use depending on what you're trying to describe.

뜨겁다 This means that some physical object is "hot" to the touch — such as a light bulb, a beverage, or a car engine.

커피가 너무 뜨거워서 못 마시고 있어요.

"I am not drinking the coffee because it's too hot."

덥다 This means that your body feels "hot" — due to the weather, the air, or from wearing too many clothes.

오늘 날씨가 어제보다 더워요.

"Today's weather is hotter than yesterday."

차갑다 This means that some physical object is "cold" to the touch — such as food that's been in the refrigerator, ice, or a snowball.

오늘 아침에 차가운 커피를 마셨어요.
"I drank cold coffee this morning."

춥다 This means that your body feels "cold" — due to it being winter, a cold breeze, or from not wearing enough clothes.

여름은 덥고 겨울은 추워요.
"Summer is hot, and winter is cold."

One exception is for 뜨겁다. When the weather is *scorching hot*, it's okay to use 뜨겁다 to describe it. In this way, it's almost like the weather is so hot that you can feel it. This is not a common usage, but is acceptable.

정말 뜨거운 날씨네요.
"It's such hot weather."

⋯ BONUS EXAMPLES ⋯

ⓧ 날씨가 너무 차가워요.

✓ 날씨가 너무 추워요.

Meaning "The weather is so cold."

ⓧ 요즘 너무 차가워서 밖에 안 나가요.

✓ 요즘 너무 추워서 밖에 안 나가요.

Meaning "It's so cold these days that I don't go outside."

ⓧ 어젯밤에 너무 뜨거워서 잠을 못 잤어요.

✓ 어젯밤에 너무 더워서 잠을 못 잤어요.

Meaning "It was so hot last night that I couldn't sleep."

You're Wearing Clothes Wrong

⊗ **THE WRONG WAY**

선글라스를 입고 싶어요.

"I want to wear sunglasses."

⊘ **THE RIGHT WAY**

선글라스를 쓰고 싶어요.

"I want to wear sunglasses."

WHY IS THIS WRONG?

There are several verbs in Korean to use for "to wear" depending on what it is you are wearing. The verb **입다** ("to wear") is only used for things that you wear around your whole body, such as pants and shirts. This sentence sounds like you're trying to put the sunglasses on your body, not your eyes.

NEVER MAKE THIS MISTAKE AGAIN

The verb for "to wear" that you should use depends on what it is and where you're wearing it. Here are some of the most common verbs you should know:

입다 This is used for things that you can wear around your whole body — such as pants and a shirt.

이 셔츠 입어 봐요.

"Try on this shirt."

신다 This is used for things that you can wear on your feet — such as socks and shoes.

신발을 신었어요.

"I wore my shoes."

쓰다 This is used for things that you can wear on your head — such as glasses, a mask, or a hat.

교실에서 모자 쓰면 안 돼요.
"You shouldn't wear a hat in the classroom."

매다 This is used for things that you can wear with straps — such as a backpack or seatbelt.

안전벨트를 매 주세요.
"Please wear your seatbelt."

끼다 This is used for things that you can wear on your hands — such as rings and gloves.

손가락이 두꺼워서 반지를 낄 수가 없어요.
"My finger is big, so I can't wear a ring."

차다 This is used for things that you can wear on your wrist, or attach to your body — such as a watch or bracelet.

손목시계를 찼어요.
"I put on my wristwatch."

두르다 This is used for things that you can wear around your neck — such as a scarf. Or alternatively, you can just use the verb 하다.

목도리 두르는 방법 아세요?
목도리 하는 방법 아세요?
"Do you know how to wear a scarf?"

They're My Parents, Not Ours

⊗ **THE WRONG WAY**

내 엄마는 요리를 잘하셔.

"My mom cooks well."

⊘ **THE RIGHT WAY**

우리 엄마는 요리를 잘하셔.

"My mom cooks well."

WHY IS THIS WRONG?

Saying **내 엄마** (or **제 엄마**) is like saying "my mom and not yours." Instead, the word **우리** should be used with family members, which means that person is a part of **your** family.

NEVER MAKE THIS MISTAKE AGAIN

When you are referring to something or someone that **belongs to you**, you can use the word 내 (for casual speech) or 제 (for formal speech).

내 신발 어디 있어?

"Where are my shoes?"

이 사람은 제 친구예요.

"This person is my friend."

However, when used with family members, or something that isn't solely owned by yourself, use 우리 ("we," "our").

우리 아빠는…

"My dad…"

The same goes for pets, which are seen as being owned together with your other family members (or whoever lives at your house).

제 강아지... ⊗
우리 강아지... ✓
"My puppy…"

You could also use 우리 집 ("our house") and the animal type for referring to animals if you want to **emphasize** that the animal is owned by everyone in the house.

우리 집 강아지...
"My house's puppy…"
"My family's puppy…"

And the same goes for your home (우리 집), your school (우리 학교), and your country (우리 나라).

제 나라는 눈이 안 와요. ⊗
*우리 나라는 눈이 안 와요. ✓
"It doesn't snow in my country."

* Note the spacing and meaning difference between 우리 나라 ("my country") and 우리나라 ("South Korea").

One more word is 저희, another word for 우리 used in **humble speech** — for when you want to speak extra politely to someone. Its usage is the same.

우리 집
= 저희 집
"My house…"

⊗　내 아빠는 저기 계셔.

✓　우리 아빠는 저기 계셔.

Meaning　　"My dad is over there."

CHAPTER 28

Hello And Goodbye

⊗ **THE WRONG WAY**

A: **안녕히 계세요.**

"Goodbye."

B: **네, 안녕히 계세요.**

"Yes, goodbye."

⊘ **THE RIGHT WAY**

A: **안녕히 계세요.**

"Goodbye."

B: **네, 안녕히 가세요.**

"Yes, goodbye."

WHY IS THIS WRONG?

안녕히 계세요 means "Stay in peace," so replying with this after someone says it to you would mean that neither of you are going anywhere.

NEVER MAKE THIS MISTAKE AGAIN

You can say goodbye with either 안녕히 계세요 or 안녕히 가세요.

안녕히 계세요 is used when you're leaving and someone else is staying. This phrase literally means "Stay in peace."

안녕히 가세요 is used when you're staying and someone else is leaving. This phrase literally means "Go in peace."

Although both people can say 안녕히 가세요 to each other as they both leave, if one person is staying, then the other person must use 안녕히 계세요 to him or her.

Note that both of these phrases are very polite, and you shouldn't use them to close friends. However, there's a right and wrong way to make these phrases casual.

안녕히 가요. ⊗
잘 가(요). ⊘

Goodbye ("go well").

안녕히 있어. ⊗
잘 있어(요). ⊘
먼저 갈게(요). ⊘
Goodbye ("I'll go first").

You can also just say 안녕 ("Bye!") to someone who's staying, or any other greeting.
There is no single common casual version of 안녕히 계세요.

To the person who stays:

⊗ 안녕히 가세요.

⊘ 안녕히 계세요.

Meaning "Goodbye."

⊗ 잘 가요.

⊘ 잘 있어요.

Meaning "Goodbye."

⊗ 잘 가.

⊘ 잘 있어.

Meaning "Goodbye."

Coming And Going

⊗ **THE WRONG WAY**

저는 심심할 때 걸어가는 걸 좋아해요.

"I like walking when I'm bored."

⊘ **THE RIGHT WAY**

저는 심심할 때 걷는 걸 좋아해요.

"I like walking when I'm bored."

WHY IS THIS WRONG?

Here, using **걸어가다** ("to walk somewhere") sounds like you enjoy walking *somewhere* and not walking *in general*. Perhaps you specifically enjoy walking to school, but the sentence can be vague without stating that.

NEVER MAKE THIS MISTAKE AGAIN

가다 and 오다 can be attached to action verbs that show motion (such as walking, running, or leaving) to show the direction that motion is going. With 가다, it's used to show that the motion goes *away from* the speaker, while 오다 shows that the motion is *coming toward* the speaker.

빨리 들어가세요.

"Go in quickly (there)."

빨리 들어오세요.

"Come in quickly (here)."

걷다 ("to walk") means "to walk *in general*," while 걸어가다 means "to walk (somewhere)." In the same way, 걸어오다 means "to walk (here)."

Use verbs without 가다 or 오다 whenever you do not need to specify a location.

집까지 걸어갈 수 있어요?

"Can you walk to your house (there)?"

여기까지 걸어왔어요?

"Did you walk all the way here?"

비도 오는데 걸어왔어요?

"You walked in this rain?"

···· BONUS EXAMPLES ····································

ⓧ 걸어가기 운동 할까요?

ⓥ 걷기 운동 할까요?

Meaning   "Shall we go walking?"

ⓧ 걸어가서 얼마나 걸려요?

ⓥ 걸어서 얼마나 걸려요?

Meaning   "How long does it take on foot?"

ⓧ 저희 아기는 이제 걸어갈 수 있어요.

ⓥ 저희 아기는 이제 걸을 수 있어요.

Meaning   "My baby can now walk."

CHAPTER 30

Leave Now And Come Back

⊗ **THE WRONG WAY**

A: 장 보러 갔다 올게.

"I'll go grocery shopping."

B: 잘 가!

"Goodbye!"

⊘ **THE RIGHT WAY**

A: 장 보러 갔다 올게.

"I'll go grocery shopping."

B: 다녀와!

"Okay, goodbye (and come back again)!"

WHY IS THIS WRONG?

Saying "goodbye" with **잘 가(요)** or **안녕히 가세요** means that you don't expect to see that person for a while. If your roommate is going to be returning shortly, this phrase would sound awkward.

NEVER MAKE THIS MISTAKE AGAIN

In Korean, telling someone to leave is often done by telling them to go and then come back again. Only telling someone to leave means that you don't expect to be seeing them again soon. For example, if your roommate announces they're going to the grocery store, replying 잘 가 means that you don't expect to see them for a long time.

If you want to tell someone to leave, but expect or hope to see them again soon, use a different phrase.

다녀와(요) This phrase literally means "go and then come back." In more polite situations, you can also use 다녀오세요.

In addition, you also say that you'll **go somewhere** and then come back when announcing that you're leaving. This clarifies that you're only going to be leaving for a short time.

다녀올게요!
"Goodbye (and I'll be back)!"

빨리 갔다 올게요.
"I'll go and come back quickly."

친구 집에 갔다 올게요.
"I'll go to a friend's house (and then come back)."

· · · BONUS EXAMPLES ·

⊗ (To your father who leaves for work)
안녕히 가세요.

✓ 안녕히 다녀오세요.

Meaning

"Have a good day at work!"
(Lit. "Please go and come
back safely.")

⊗ (To your parents when you leave for
school) 학교 가겠습니다.

✓ 학교 다녀오겠습니다.

Meaning

"I'm off to school!"

⊗ (To your friend who is going on
vacation) 잘 가.

✓ 잘 다녀와.

Meaning

"Have a nice trip!"

What Time Is It?

⊗ **THE WRONG WAY**

지금 시간이 뭐예요?

"What is the time now?"

⊘ **THE RIGHT WAY**

지금 몇 시예요?

"What time is it now?"

WHY IS THIS WRONG?

시간 means "time," as in the **concept** of time or the amount of time you have or need. If you were to ask someone this, you'd better hope they're a physicist.

NEVER MAKE THIS MISTAKE AGAIN

To ask what time it is, you'll need to specifically ask what hour of the day it is. You can do this using 몇 ("how many") and the counter 시 ("o'clock").

몇 시예요?
"What time is it?"

To reply, you can say the hour using pure Korean numbers and the counter 시.

1 o'clock → 한 시
6 o'clock → 여섯 시
10 o'clock → 열 시

Note that 시 is the counter for "o'clock," but 시간 is a **different** counter for "hours" (such as when you want to say you studied for two hours). These two counters should not be mixed up.

한 시예요.
"It's 1 o'clock."

한 시간이에요.
"It's one hour."

To say the minutes, use Sino-Korean numbers and the counter 분.

1:30 → 1시 30분 ("한 시 삼십 분")
5:54 → 5시 54분 ("다섯 시 오십사 분")
12:02 → 12시 2분 (열두 시 이 분")

To say the seconds, use Sino-Korean numbers and the counter 초.

10 seconds → 10초 ("십 초")
33 seconds → 33초 ("삼십삼 초")

• • • BONUS EXAMPLES •

(×) 시간 있어요?

(✓) 몇 시예요?

Meaning   "Do you have the time?"

(×) 몇 시간에 일 끝나요?

(✓) 몇 시에 일 끝나요?

Meaning   "What time do you finish work?"

(×) 무슨 시간에 왔어요?

(✓) 몇 시에 왔어요?

Meaning   "What time did you get here?"

What Day Is It?

오늘 무슨 날이에요?

"What day is it today?"

오늘 무슨 요일이에요?

"What day of the week is today?"

WHY IS THIS WRONG?

The adjective **무슨** ("what") and **날** ("day") means "what day," but **날** doesn't mean the day of the week — it's just *a day* in general. Asking **무슨 날** would be like asking *what kind of* day it was, as if the day was some sort of special occasion.

NEVER MAKE THIS MISTAKE AGAIN

무슨 is still used to ask what day of the *week* it is, but only together with 요일 ("day of the week"). You can use 무슨 요일 in whatever sentence structure you'd like to ask the day of the week.

If you ask this, someone will likely respond with which day of the week it is.

오늘은 화요일이에요.
"Today is Tuesday."

Let's review the days of the week:

월요일 → "Monday"
화요일 → "Tuesday"
수요일 → "Wednesday"
목요일 → "Thursday"
금요일 → "Friday"
토요일 → "Saturday"

일요일 → "Sunday"

To ask which day of the **_month_** it is, use 며칠.

오늘 며칠이에요?
"Which day (of the month) is it today?"
"What's the date today?"

To reply with the date, use a Sino-Korean number together with the counter 일 ("day").

1st → 1일 ("일 일")
5th → 5일 ("오 일")
31st → 31일 ("삼십일 일")

···· **BONUS EXAMPLES** ···

⊗ 무슨 날에 발레 학원 가요?

✓ 무슨 요일에 발레 학원 가요?

Meaning "Which day do you go to your ballet class?"

⊗ 그 박물관은 무슨 일에 쉬어요?

✓ 그 박물관은 무슨 요일에 쉬어요?

Meaning "On which day is the museum closed?"

⊗ 올해 크리스마스는 몇 일이에요?

✓ 올해 크리스마스는 무슨 요일이에요?

Meaning "Which day is Christmas this year?"

CHAPTER 33

Organizing Your Time

⊗ **THE WRONG WAY**

오늘 저는 3시 오후에 점심을 먹었어요.
"Today I ate lunch at 3 o'clock
in the afternoon."

⊘ **THE RIGHT WAY**

오늘 저는 오후 3시에 점심을 먹었어요.
"Today I ate lunch at 3 o'clock
in the afternoon."

WHY IS THIS WRONG?

Time in Korean is organized with the largest units on the left and the smallest units on the right. When things aren't arranged the correct way, a sentence can feel out of order.

NEVER MAKE THIS MISTAKE AGAIN

Organize time from the largest unit (such as years) to the smallest (such as seconds), going from left to right.

Saying the year, month, and day always goes in that order.

6월 15일 1986년 ⊗
1986년 6월 15일 ⊘
"June 15th, 1986"

Saying the general day (such as today or tomorrow), the time of day (such as the morning or afternoon), and the hour always goes in that order.

내일 8시 저녁에 만나요. ⊗
내일 저녁 8시에 만나요. ⊘
"Let's meet tomorrow evening at 8 o'clock."

Note that the general day (such as today or tomorrow) will usually come toward the beginning of a sentence, either before or after the subject. In casual spoken usage, it can come later in the sentence, but it will sound as though the speaker forgot to say it, and the sentence will sound much less natural.

저는 시간이 없어요 오늘. **(less natural)**
저는 오늘 시간이 없어요. **(more natural)**
"I don't have time today."

Saying the hour, minute, and second always goes in that order.

6시 30분 30초
"6:30 and 30 seconds"

What's Your Name?

⊘ THE RIGHT WAY

할아버지! 성함이 어떻게 되세요?

"(Grandfather!) What's your name?"

WHY IS THIS WRONG?

이름이 뭐예요? does mean "What is your name?" However, this phrase is inappropriate to use toward someone much older than you. In this case, to a **할아버지**, it would sound rude.

NEVER MAKE THIS MISTAKE AGAIN

There are a few ways to ask someone's name, and the one you should use will depend on who you are asking.

성함이 어떻게 되세요?
"What's your name?"

성함 is an *honorific noun* that means "name." Using 성함 instead of 이름 ("name") shows extra respect toward the person who you're asking. However, only use 성함 for another person's name, and not for your own name, to avoid sounding awkward.

제 성함은 빌리예요. ⊗
제 이름은 빌리예요. ⊘
"My name's Billy."

어떻게 되세요? literally means "How is it?" It can also be loosely translated to "Tell me about." In this way, you can think of this phrase as meaning "Tell me about your name." You can also use 어떻게 되세요? to ask someone about their family or hobbies, among other topics.

이름이 어떻게 되세요?
"What's your name?"

The phrase 어떻게 되세요 can also be used with 이름 when speaking with someone who you don't need to show extra politeness toward. As this phrase contains the -세요 honorific ending, it is still polite in general, but should not be used to anyone who is much older than you.

이름이 어떻게 돼요?
"What's your name?"

This uses 돼요 instead of 되세요, and should only be used in *informal* situations, such as when making new friends or meeting people who appear younger than you.

이름이 뭐예요?
"What's your name?"

This phrase is also acceptable to use in informal situations, but is slightly less polite. This would be fine to use toward young kids.

이름이 뭐야?
"What's your name?"

Because this phrase uses *casual speech*, it should not be used toward anyone who you want to show respect toward — even perhaps young kids, depending on the situation. For this reason, this one is the least used of all the phrases. Only kids would say this to each other.

CHAPTER 35

Saying Your Age Wrong

⊗ **THE WRONG WAY**

저는 이십 년이에요.

"I'm 20 years old."

⊘ **THE RIGHT WAY**

저는 스무 살이에요.

"I'm 20 years old."

WHY IS THIS WRONG?

While 년 is used to count years, it can't be used to count a **person's** years —
someone's age. To count age, the counter 살 must be used together with pure
Korean numbers. This sentence would sound like, "As for me, it's been 20 years." It
would not mean that you are 20 years old.

NEVER MAKE THIS MISTAKE AGAIN

As we learned previously, there are two number systems in Korean — pure Korean
numbers and Sino-Korean numbers. Each system will be used for a different
purpose, such as counting people or objects.

To count a person's years — how old they are — use pure Korean numbers together
with the **counter** 살. Remember that the numbers 1 to 4 and 20 will change when
used directly before a counter.

3 years old / 3살 ("세 살")
5 years old / 5살 ("다섯 살")
21 years old / 21살 ("스물한 살")
40 years old / 40살 ("마흔 살")

Pure Korean numbers are most often used up until 40 (마흔) or 50 (쉰). Beyond
that, it's common to simply switch back to the Sino-Korean number system — even
when counting years. However, when you do so, switch the counter 살 to a different

counter 세.

50살 ("쉰 살" or "오십 세")

Also, note that Korea uses a different age system than the rest of the world — you'll be either one or two years older in Korean age. To calculate your Korean age, take the current year and subtract your birthday year. Then, add one year on top of that.

To count years (in general), use Sino-Korean numbers together with 년 ("year").

3 years / 3년 ("삼 년")
21 years / 21년 ("이십일 년")

The counter 년 can also be used when talking about inanimate objects that are a certain number of years old. When used in this way, attach the verb 되다 ("to become") and conjugate it. For example, if you wanted to say that a car is 10 years old, you can say 이 차는 십 년 됐어요 ("This car is 10 years old."). Or if you wanted to say that it is a 10-year-old car, you can say 이건 십 년 된 차예요 ("This is a 10-year-old car.").

이 건물은 100년 됐어요.
"This building is 100 years old."

이거 500년 된 나무예요.
"This is a 500-year-old tree."

· · · **BONUS EXAMPLES** ·

ⓧ 이제 1년 됐어요.

✓ 이제 한 살 됐어요.

Meaning "He/She now turned one."

CHAPTER 36

How Old Are You?

⊗ THE WRONG WAY

할머니, 몇 살이에요?

"Grandmother, how old are you?"

⊘ THE RIGHT WAY

할머니, 연세가 어떻게 되세요?

"Grandmother, how old are you?"

WHY IS THIS WRONG?

It would be inappropriate and rude to ask someone who is much older than you their age using **몇 살**.

NEVER MAKE THIS MISTAKE AGAIN

There are a few ways to ask someone's age, and the one you should use will depend on who you are asking.

연세가 어떻게 되세요?

"How old are you?"

연세 is an **honorific noun** that means "age," and shows extra respect toward the person who you're referring to. Remember to only use 연세 when talking about someone else's age, not your own.

나이가 어떻게 되세요?

나이가 어떻게 돼요?

"How old are you?"

Using 나이 ("age") is a step down from 연세, but is acceptable outside of formal situations and with people who are not much older than you. You can use 어떻게 되세요 to be more polite, or 어떻게 돼요, depending on how polite you want to be.

몇 살이에요?

몇 살이야?

"How old are you?"

몇 살 ("how many years old") is only used when speaking to someone who is much younger than you. It should also be avoided in any polite or formal situation. As such, it's okay to use when referring to younger children.

• • • BONUS EXAMPLES •

Inappropriate/Impolite	Appropriate/Polite	Meaning
부모님이 몇 살이에요?	부모님 연세가 어떻게 되세요?	"How old are your parents?"
할머니 나이가 여든이에요.	할머니 연세가 여든이세요.	"(My/His/Her) grandmother is 80 years old."
저희 할아버지 나이가 많아요.	저희 할아버지 연세가 많으세요.	"My grandfather is very old."

Speak Casually To Yourself

⊗ **THE WRONG WAY**

저는 할 수 있다!

"I can do it!"

⊘ **THE RIGHT WAY**

나는 할 수 있다!

"I can do it!"

WHY IS THIS WRONG?

It's important to use the right amount of politeness depending on who you're talking with or talking about — this shows respect. However, when speaking to or about yourself, there's no need to speak respectfully, and doing so will actually cause your Korean to sound awkward.

NEVER MAKE THIS MISTAKE AGAIN

When speaking to yourself about yourself (even when around others who might be listening), there's no need to speak using polite forms. This is because politeness forms are used when speaking politely to and about other people — not yourself.

When you're walking down the street with someone whom you would normally speak politely to, feel free to speak casually toward yourself about yourself. For example, you might be walking outside in freezing cold temperatures, in which case you can say to yourself, 아, 진짜 춥다! ("Ah, it's so cold!") without worrying about using the 요 form or some other polite form of speech.

아, 진짜 추워요! ⊗
아, 진짜 춥다! ⊘
"Ah, it's so cold!"

Note that this is only when you're not speaking directly toward someone, or else it could be understood that you're speaking to them and not to yourself.

Remember that 저 itself is also polite, so only use 나 when talking to yourself.

저 왜 이러지? ⊗
나 왜 이러지? ⊘
"What's wrong with me?"

In addition, avoid using any honorific nouns when talking about yourself — whether you're talking to yourself or with others. This includes the honorific nouns 분 (counter for "people"), 댁 ("house"), 성함 ("name"), and 연세 ("age"), among others. For example, although 명 and 분 are both counters for people, use only 명 when talking about yourself or your group and 분 when speaking about others.

A: 몇 분이세요?
"How many are you?"

B: 세 분이요. ⊗
B: 세 명이요. ⊘
"There are three of us."

저희 댁은 저기 있어요. ⊗
저희 집은 저기 있어요. ⊘
"My house is over there."

⊗ 제 성함은 제니퍼입니다.
⊘ 제 이름은 제니퍼입니다.

Meaning   "My name is Jennifer."

⊗ 제가 왜 여기 있지?
⊘ 내가 왜 여기 있지?

Meaning   "Why am I here?"

CHAPTER 38

What Do You Think?

⊗ THE WRONG WAY

뭐 생각해요?

"What do you think?"

⊘ THE RIGHT WAY

어떻게 생각해요?

"What do you think?"

WHY IS THIS WRONG?

뭐 means "what," but asking someone what they're thinking with this word sounds more like you're asking them "what" they're thinking about, and not what they think about something or what their opinion is. In addition, this phrase would also be an unnatural way to say that as well.

NEVER MAKE THIS MISTAKE AGAIN

To ask someone "what" they think about something — their opinion — you need to actually ask them "how" they think about it. The word for "how" is 어떻게.

어떻게 생각하세요?
"What (how) do you think?"

To be more polite (such as when not talking to close friends), you can also use 하세요 at the end. If you want to be more specific and ask what someone thinks **about something**, you can add "about" before this form.

About: Noun + -에 대해(서)

To use this form, attach -에 대해(서) after a noun; the 서 is **optional**.

그 영화에 대해서 어떻게 생각하세요?
"What do you think about that movie?"

이 아이디어에 대해 어떻게 생각하세요?
"What do you think about this idea?"

Another quicker way to ask someone what they think about something is to directly ask them **how** something is.

How: Noun + 어때(요)?

To use this form, attach -어때(요) after a noun; you can remove 요 when speaking with close friends.

이 책 어때요?
"How is this book?"

이 영화 어때요?
"How is this movie?"

Note that 어때(요) and 어떠세요 literally mean "how is it," so the sentence 이 영화 어때요? could also translate as "How about this movie?" — as in "Shall we watch this movie?" Whether you're suggesting to see a certain movie or asking about it will be clear by the context.

・・・ **BONUS EXAMPLES** ・・・・・・・・・・・・・・・・・・・・・・・・・・・

⊗ 무슨 생각해요?

✓ 어떻게 생각해요?

Meaning   "What do you think?"

⊗ 무엇을 생각해요?

✓ 어떻게 생각해요?

Meaning   "What do you think?"

The Plain Form

⊗ THE WRONG WAY

저는 한국어를 공부하고 있어요.
"I am studying Korean."

⊘ THE RIGHT WAY

나는 한국어를 공부하고 있다.
"I am studying Korean."

WHY IS THIS WRONG?

When spoken, this example sentence is perfect. However, when written in an essay, this sentence would be awkward and inappropriate.

NEVER MAKE THIS MISTAKE AGAIN

When writing an essay or scribbling in your diary, use the *plain form*. The *plain form* is used in several grammar forms, and is useful to master — not to mention essential for writing down your thoughts. While the *plain form* would be too casual if spoken (except to close friends in certain situations), it is proper when writing something that has *no intended audience*. If you don't know how to address the people who will be reading your writing, use the *plain form*. This is why it's found in news articles, essays, and reports.

Plain Form: Action Verb Stem + -(느)ㄴ다

For action verbs in the *present tense*, take the verb stem and attach -는 if it ends in a *consonant*, or attach -ㄴ if it ends in a *vowel*. Then attach 다. Verb stems ending in ㄹ will also lose their ㄹ.

먹다 → 먹는다
공부하다 → 공부한다
만들다 → 만든다

For descriptive verbs in the *present tense*, no additional conjugation is necessary.

있다 → 있다
친절하다 → 친절하다

For all verbs in the *past tense*, conjugate to the 요 form in past tense, and remove any additional 요 form conjugation at the end (such as -아요, -어요, etc.). Then attach 다.

공부하다 → 공부했어요 → 공부했다
어렵다 → 어려웠어요 → 어려웠다
-이다 → -이었어요 or -였어요 → -이었다 or -였다

Note that -이다 will become -이었다 after a consonant and -였다 after a *vowel*.

For all verbs in the *future tense*, conjugate either the -(으)ㄹ 것이다 ending (shortened to -(으)ㄹ 거다) or the -겠다 ending. No additional conjugation is necessary.

요리하다 → 요리할 것이다, 요리할 거다, or 요리하겠다
먹다 → 먹을 것이다, 먹을 거다, or 먹겠다

One more thing: when used in writing, use 나 instead of 저. Although 나 is only spoken in *casual speech*, it is required in writing. Using 저 would sound overly polite for writing where the reader is unknown.

저는 파스타를 만들고 싶다. ⊗
나는 파스타를 만들고 싶다. ⊘
"I want to make pasta."

· · · BONUS EXAMPLES ·

When written in an essay:

		Meaning	"I went to school today."
Inappropriate	저는 오늘 학교에 갔어요.		
Appropriate	나는 오늘 학교에 갔다.		

CHAPTER 40

Explaining What You Think

⊗ **THE WRONG WAY**

저는 좋아 생각해요.

"I think it's good."

⊘ **THE RIGHT WAY**

저는 좋다고 생각해요.

"I think it's good."

WHY IS THIS WRONG?

While this example would make sense, it's completely grammatically wrong and would sound strange. You'd need to use a different form of 좋다 ('to be good"), such as the *plain form*, to express your opinion.

NEVER MAKE THIS MISTAKE AGAIN

To express your thoughts, use the *plain form* together with -고 and 생각하다 ("to think").

plain form + -고 생각하다

To express your thoughts or say what you're thinking, first conjugate the *plain form*. Next, attach -고 directly to the end of the *plain form*, and conjugate the verb 생각하다.

좋다고 생각해요.
"I think it's good."

오늘은 아주 덥다고 생각해요.
"I think today is very hot."

그 사람도 한국말을 잘한다고 생각해요.
"I think that person can also speak Korean well."

Note that -이다("to be") is irregular and conjugates to -이라고 after a **consonant** or
-라고 after a **vowel** when used with this specific form. The same is true of 아니다,
which becomes 아니라고.

경은 씨가 좋은 사람이라고 생각해요.
"I think Kyeong-eun is a good person."

그 사람이 학생이라고 생각해요.
"I think that person is a student."

그 사람이 빌리라고 생각해요.
"I think that person is Billy."

그 사람이 빌리가 아니라고 생각해요.
"I think that person's not Billy."

그 일은 다른 사람이 할 거라고 생각해요.
"I think another person will do that work."

제가 혼자 다 먹을 수 있을 거라고 생각해요.
"I think I will be able to eat it all by myself."

・・ **BONUS EXAMPLES** ・・・・・・・

ⓧ 저는 재밌어 생각해요.

✓ 저는 재밌다고 생각해요.

Meaning "I think it's fun."

ⓧ 저는 어려워 생각해요.

✓ 저는 어렵다고 생각해요.

Meaning "I think it's difficult."

CAN YOU SPOT WHAT'S WRONG WITH THIS SENTENCE?

저는 새로운 자동차를 필요해요.

✓ See Chapter 45

CHAPTER 41

How To Use -에 And -에서

ⓧ **THE WRONG WAY**

저는 지금 한국에 공부하고 있어요.

"I'm studying in Korea now."

⊘ **THE RIGHT WAY**

저는 지금 한국에서 공부하고 있어요.

"I am studying in Korea now."

WHY IS THIS WRONG?

The particle -에 can be used to show the location of something, but not *where* something happens. Instead, -에서 needs to be used whenever there's an action verb.

NEVER MAKE THIS MISTAKE AGAIN

The particle -에 means "to," "in," and "at" in English.

저는 한국에 가고 싶어요.

"I want to go to Korea."

저희 집에는 냉장고가 없어요.

"There isn't a refrigerator in/at our house."

현우 씨는 사무실에 있어요.

"Hyunwoo is in/at the office."

This can cause some confusion with the particle -에서, which can mean "at." -에서 can be used to show the location where something happens. Use -에서 whenever you want to show the location where an *action verb* happens.

현우 씨는 사무실에서 일해요.

"Hyunwoo works at the office."

백화점에서 컴퓨터를 샀어요.
"I bought a computer at the department store."

집에서 설거지했어요.
"I did the dishes at home."

Note that the action verb 살다 ("to live") is an exception, and can use either -에 or -에서.

한국에서 살고 있어요.
한국에 살고 있어요.
"I'm living in Korea."

The particle -에서 can also be used to mean "from," although this usage is unrelated to its confusion with -에.

저는 미국에서 왔어요.
"I'm from America."

학교에서 집까지 뛰어갔어요.
"I ran home from school."

BONUS EXAMPLES

ⓧ 집에서 언제 가요?

✓ 집에 언제 가요?

Meaning — "When are you going home?"

ⓧ 어디에 공부해요?

✓ 어디에서 공부해요?

Meaning — "Where do you study?"

CHAPTER 42

You're Welcome

⊗ **THE WRONG WAY**

천만에요.

"You're welcome."

⊘ **THE RIGHT WAY**

아니에요.

"You're welcome."

WHY IS THIS WRONG?

천만에요 is an old-fashioned way to say "You're welcome." There are better ways to say this.

NEVER MAKE THIS MISTAKE AGAIN

There are several ways to say "you're welcome" depending on the situation.

천만에요 This is an older expression that literally means "not at all," and it is no longer commonly used. You might hear it from time to time used by older people, but it's not recommended.

아니에요 or 아니야 These expressions both mean "No, it isn't." You can use 아니에요 in any polite situation, and 아니야 with close friends, but neither is formal. If you are in a formal situation, you could say 아닙니다, which is a combination of 아니다 and the formal ending -(스)ㅂ니다. Because it comes from 아니다 ("to not be"), it can be used whenever you want to politely deny what someone has said, such as responding to compliments. In this way, it's like saying "No, you don't need to say that."

A: 정말 감사합니다!
"Thank you!"

B: 아니에요.

"You're welcome."

A: 한국말 너무 잘하시네요!

"Your Korean is so good!"

B: 아니에요.

"Ah, no."

뭘요 This expression is not formal, but is polite. Its literal meaning is "what," and it can be used in a similar way as saying "No problem" or "It's nothing." For example, you could use this expression to respond to someone saying "thank you" after you've done them a favor.

A: 오늘 도와줘서 고마워요.

"Thanks for helping today."

B: 뭘요.

"No problem."

"It's nothing."

에이 This short sound can be added before 아니에요, 아니야, or 뭘요. Adding this will make the expression sound more friendly, but less formal or polite. As such, it should only be used with friends and acquaintances.

에이, 뭘요!

"Eh, it's nothing!"

CHAPTER 43

Transitive And Intransitive Verbs

⊗ **THE WRONG WAY**

저는 미국에 큰 아파트를 있어요.

"I have a big apartment in America."

⊘ **THE RIGHT WAY**

저는 미국에 큰 아파트가 있어요.

"I have a big apartment in America."

WHY IS THIS WRONG?

있어요 can't take a direct object of its own because it basically means "exist".

NEVER MAKE THIS MISTAKE AGAIN

There are two types of action verbs in Korean — transitive verbs and intransitive verbs. These terms aren't important to memorize, but it is important to know how each verb can be used with particles.

Transitive verbs are all verbs in Korean that can affect a noun. These verbs use the *object marker*, -을/를, to show what noun they're affecting.

먹다 "to eat"
피자가 먹다 → "pizza eats (something)" ⊗
피자를 먹다 → "to eat pizza" ⊘

저는 피자가 먹어요. ⊗
저는 피자를 먹어요. ⊘
"I eat pizza."

Intransitive verbs are all verbs in Korean that do not affect a noun. These verbs cannot use the *object marker*, -을/를.

있다 "to exist"
피자를 있다 → "to exist pizza" ⊗
피자가 있다 → "pizza exists" ⊘

저는 피자를 있어요. ⊗
저는 피자가 있어요. ⊘
"I have pizza."

Again, you do not need to learn the terms "transitive verb" and "intransitive verbs"
— simply knowing whether a verb can directly affect a noun or not is enough. If you
know that, then you can know whether that verb uses the **object marker** or not.

Note that all descriptive verbs are automatically intransitive verbs, as they don't do
anything to nouns, and therefore, cannot use the **object marker**.

한국 드라마를 좋아요. ⊗
한국 드라마가 좋아요. ⊘
"I like Korean dramas."

한국어를 정말 재미있어요! ⊗
한국어가 정말 재미있어요! ⊘
"Korean is really fun!"

· · BONUS EXAMPLES ·

⊗ 사람을 있어요.

⊘ 사람이 있어요.

Meaning "There is a person."

⊗ 저는 한국이 많이 좋아해요.

⊘ 저는 한국이 많이 좋아요.

⊘ 저는 한국을 많이 좋아해요.

Meaning "I like Korea a lot."

What Do You Want?

새로운 자동차를 원해요.

"I want a new car."

새로운 자동차를 갖고 싶어요.

새로운 자동차가 갖고 싶어요.

"I want to have a new car."

WHY IS THIS WRONG?

원하다 ("to want") is not commonly used to directly say that you want **something**. Using this verb can sound like your sentence is a direct translation of an English sentence.

NEVER MAKE THIS MISTAKE AGAIN

원하다 literally means "to want," but it can sound too direct. There is a much more natural way to say that you want **something**. To say that you want to **have** something, use 가지고 싶다 ("to want to have"). The verb 가지다 means "to have," as in "to have on one's person." This is also shortened to 갖고 싶다 very often when spoken.

그 컴퓨터를 가지고 싶어요.

그 컴퓨터를 갖고 싶어요.

"I want to have that computer."

In addition to the **object marker**, -을/를, it is okay to use the **subject marker**, -이/가, to talk about what you want to have in front of 가지고 싶다 or 갖고 싶다. Doing this emphasizes what it is that you want to have.

이 카메라를 갖고 싶어요.

이 카메라가 갖고 싶어요.

"I want to have this camera."

뭐가 갖고 싶어요?

"What item do you want to have?"

To say that you want to **do** something, use a different form.

Action Verb Stem + -고 싶다

To use this form, take an action verb stem (the verb which you want to do) and attach -고 싶다 to the verb stem. Then conjugate it.

새로운 자동차를 사기를 원해요. ⓧ
새로운 자동차를 사고 싶어요. ✓
"I want to buy a new car."

한국어를 배우고 싶어요.
"I want to learn Korean."

현우 씨를 만나고 싶어요.
"I want to meet Hyunwoo."

So then when is the verb 원하다 used? While it's not used to say that you want to have something, or that you want to do something, it can be used **indirectly** — as an adjective.

제가 원하는 과자가 여기 없어요.
"The snack I want isn't here."

I Need It

⊗ **THE WRONG WAY**

저는 새로운 자동차를 필요해요.

"I need a new car."

⊘ **THE RIGHT WAY**

저는 새로운 자동차가 필요해요.

"I need a new car."

WHY IS THIS WRONG?

필요하다 is a ***descriptive verb***, and therefore, can't have an object. This sentence, while understandable, would sound awkward, like saying "I necessary a new car."

NEVER MAKE THIS MISTAKE AGAIN

필요하다: This means "to be necessary," and is ***not*** an action verb. It's not possible "to be necessary" something. Instead, something can be ***necessary***. It can be used with the ***subject marker***, -이/가, or another marker such as the ***topic marker***, -은/는, or -도, but can't be used with the ***object marker***, -을/를.

옷을 필요해요. ⊗
옷이 필요해요. ⊘
"I need clothes."

저는 남자 친구를 필요해요. ⊗
저는 남자 친구가 필요해요. ⊘
"I need a boyfriend."

Verb Stem + -아/어/여야 되다

This is another common way to say that you "need" ***to do something***. To use it, take a verb stem and conjugate it to the 요 form, removing the 요. Then attach -야 되다 and conjugate it. Or alternatively, you can instead attach -야 하다 and conjugate it (which is a bit more formal).

저는 새로운 자동차를 사야 돼요.
"I need to buy a new car."

빨리 가야 돼요.
"I have to go quickly."

오늘 꼭 일해야 돼요?
"Do you really need to work today?"

필요로 하다: This means "to require" and is an *action verb* form of 필요하다, but it's not commonly used as it sounds a bit formal. It can be used with the *object marker*.

여기에서 운전을 하려면 면허증을 필요로 합니다.
"I require a license to drive here."

· · · **BONUS EXAMPLES** ·

⊗ 젓가락을 필요해요.

✓ 젓가락이 필요해요.

Meaning "I need chopsticks."

⊗ 물을 필요해요.

✓ 물이 필요해요.

Meaning "I need water."

⊗ 도움을 필요해요.

✓ 도움이 필요해요.

Meaning "I need help."

What Will You Do?

⊗ **THE WRONG WAY**

이제 어떻게요?

"What will you do now?"

✓ **THE RIGHT WAY**

이제 어떡해요?

"What will you do now?"

WHY IS THIS WRONG?

This is half a spelling mistake and half a grammar mistake. Because **어떻게** means "how," this sentence would actually mean "Now how?"

NEVER MAKE THIS MISTAKE AGAIN

어떻게(요) and 어떡해(요) both have the same pronunciation, but different meanings.

어떻게: This adverb means "how." Originally, 어떻게 comes from the descriptive verb 어떻다, which means "to be how." This descriptive verb is also where the adjective 어떤 ("what kind of") comes from.

어떻게요?
"How?"

어떡해(요): This is an expression that literally means "What will I/you do?" It's used in a similar way as saying "Oh no." Originally, this comes from the action verb 어떡하다, which is a shortened version of 어떠하게 하다 or 어떻게 하다, meaning "how to do something."

어떡해요?
"What will you do?"

"What do I do?"

The point to take away from this lesson is that 어떻게요 and 어떡해요 are both grammatically accurate sentences, and it's important to be able to tell the difference through the context (and spelling).

A: 제가 케이크를 만들었어요.
"I made a cake."
B: 어떻게요?
"How (did you make it)?"

A: 제가 케이크를 만들었어요.
"I made a cake."
B: 어떡해요.
"Oh no! (It's probably disgusting!)"

A: 저희 아들이 시험에서 떨어졌어요.
"My son failed his test."
B: 어떻게요?
"How? (Did he not study? It's impossible.)"

A: 저희 아들이 시험에서 떨어졌어요.
"My son failed his test."
B: 어떡해요.
"Oh no! (I'm sorry to hear that!)"

··· **BONUS EXAMPLES** ·····························

⊗ 아무도 안 오면 어떻게요?

⊘ 아무도 안 오면 어떡해요?

Meaning   "What should we do if no one comes?"

Saying You're Sorry

⊗ **THE WRONG WAY**

A: 어제 저희 할아버지께서 돌아가셨어요.

"Yesterday, my grandfather passed away."

B: 정말 죄송합니다.

"I'm really sorry."

⊘ **THE RIGHT WAY**

A: 어제 저희 할아버지께서 돌아가셨어요.

"Yesterday, my grandfather passed away."

B: 상심이 크시겠어요.

"I'm so sorry to hear that."

WHY IS THIS WRONG?

죄송합니다 means that you're sorry and are apologizing for doing something. If you said this, it would mean that you were responsible for their grandfather's death — if so, then definitely turn yourself in.

NEVER MAKE THIS MISTAKE AGAIN

There are several expressions to show that you're "sorry," depending on the situation.

죄송하다 and 미안하다 You can use either of these verbs to apologize for something that you did. Technically, 죄송하다 is slightly more formal than 미안하다; because of this, these two verbs will be used when speaking at different levels of politeness. Here are some of the most common usages:

죄송합니다.
죄송해요.
"I'm sorry."

미안합니다.
미안해(요).
미안.

"I'm sorry."

Simply saying 미안 is the least sincere-sounding way of apologizing, and is closer to just saying "my bad" or "oops."

유감이다 This verb can be used to express that you're sorry to **hear** about something. However, as this verb is formal, it should not be used with friends or close acquaintances. It's also not commonly used.

유감입니다.
"I'm sorry to hear that."

상심이 크다 This phrase means that one's "grief" (상심) is "great" (크다). It is a polite expression that you can use when someone has experienced some sort of loss, and means that their grief must be great (they must be sad). It can be used together with honorifics when talking about someone else.

어떡해(요) This phrase can be used with friends or acquaintances to express that you're sorry to hear something. This comes from 어떡하다 and means "What will I/ you do?" In this way, it is used to express something similar to "Oh no."

A: 이번 시험 망했어요.
"I failed the test."
B: 어떡해요.
"I'm sorry to hear that."

· · · **BONUS EXAMPLES** · · · · · · · · · · · · · · ·

ⓧ
A: 저는 오늘도 야근이에요.
B: 미안해요. 힘들겠어요.

Meaning

A: "I work overtime today as well."
B: "I'm sorry. You must be tired."

✓
A: 저는 오늘도 야근이에요.
B: 어떡해요. 힘들겠어요.

Who's Who?

⊗ **THE WRONG WAY**

누구 했어요?

"Who did it?"

⊘ **THE RIGHT WAY**

누가 했어요?

"Who did it?"

WHY IS THIS WRONG?

누구 means "who" when used as the object of a verb. Here, the verb 하다 ("to do") would be doing something to "who," instead of "who" doing something, which would make no sense without additional context.

NEVER MAKE THIS MISTAKE AGAIN

누구 and 누가 both mean "who," depending on whether it's being used as an object or a subject in a sentence — whether some action is doing something to "who," or whether "who" is doing some action.

누구   This means "who" when it is used as an object. That means some action verb is doing something to "who." For example, when asking "who" something happened to, 누구 would be the object of that sentence. Or, you'd use 누구 when asking "who" someone met.

누구를 만났어요?

"Who did you meet?"

누가   This means "who" when it is used as a subject. This means that "who" is doing some action verb. For example, when asking "who" did something, "who" is the subject of that sentence. Or you'd use 누가 when asking "who" met someone, when not asking "who" was met. 누가 comes from 누구 and the subject marker -가 (instead of saying 누구가).

누가 만났어요?
"Who met (someone)?"

In the incorrect example, 누구 했어요 is asking "who" the action (하다) happened to, and not "who" was doing the action (하다). The sentence is therefore vague, as we don't know the subject who did the action or what the action was specifically.

선물을 누가한테 줬어요? ⊗
선물을 누구한테 줬어요? ⊘
"Who did you give the present to?"

BONUS EXAMPLES

⊗ 누구 먹었어요?

⊘ 누가 먹었어요?

Meaning   "Who ate it?"

⊗ 누구 갈 거예요?

⊘ 누가 갈 거예요?

Meaning   "Who is going?"

⊗ 누구 전화했어요?

⊘ 누가 전화했어요?

Meaning   "Who called you/us?"

Who's There?

여기 누가 계세요?

"Who's here?"

여기 누구 계세요?

"Is someone here?"

WHY IS THIS WRONG?

If you were to walk into an empty house and say this sentence, it would sound like you knew that someone is here — not that you were asking if **someone** is here in the house.

NEVER MAKE THIS MISTAKE AGAIN

누가 is a combination of 누구 ("who") and -가, the **subject marker**, so it would make sense that 여기 누가 계세요 would translate as "Who is here?" However, 누가 means that you're asking "who" is here, and not whether **someone** (or anyone) is here. If you heard some strange noises from inside of the house, you could ask 누가 계세요 to find out who it was, but it would be more natural to ask if **someone** is there since you don't know if anyone is there or not.

Not only can 누구 be used to mean "who," but it can also be used to mean "someone". In this way, 누구 can be used as "who" and as a shorter version of 누군 가 ("someone").

어제 누구 만났어요.
"I met someone yesterday."

In the same way as 누구 can be used to mean "someone," 뭐 ("what") can also be used as a shorter version of 뭔가 ("something"), and 어디 ("where") can be used as a shorter version of 어딘가 ("somewhere").

이미 뭐 먹었어요.
"I already ate something."

어디 간 것 같아요.
"I think she went somewhere."

Note that when using 누구, 뭐, and 어디 in this manner, put emphasis on the verb in the sentence. If you put emphasis on the words 누구, 뭐, or 어디, then it will instead sound like you are saying the normal words "who," "what," and "where."

뭐 했어요?
"What did you do?"

뭐 **했어요**?
"Did you do something?"

· **BONUS EXAMPLES** ·

누가	누구
누가 왔다 갔어요? "Who stopped by here?"	누구 왔다 갔어요? "Did someone stop by here?"
누가 다쳤어요? "Who got hurt?"	누구 다쳤어요? "Did someone get hurt?"
누가 불렀어요? "Who called out for me?"	누구 불렀어요? "Did you call out for someone?"

This And That

이것 음식 맛있어요.

"This food is delicious."

이 음식 맛있어요.

"This food is delicious."

WHY IS THIS WRONG?

이것 means "this thing" and is a noun — it cannot be attached directly to another noun. This sentence would therefore translate as "This thing food is delicious."

NEVER MAKE THIS MISTAKE AGAIN

Saying "this" and "that" depends on how the word is being used — as a noun or an adjective. Adjectives are used directly before a noun, while nouns cannot be. Let's cover the three adjective and three nouns that we'll need to translate these words.

이: This is an **adjective** and means "this." It's used whenever what you're talking about is close to you — the speaker — but far from the person you're talking with — the listener.

이 영화를 좋아해요.
"I like this movie."

이것/이거: This is a **noun** and means "this (thing)." It's used in the same cases as 이.

이는 아주 좋아요. ⓧ
이거 아주 좋아요. ✓
"This is very good."

그: This is an **adjective** and means "that." It's used whenever what you're talking about is far from you — the speaker — but close to the person you're talking with - the listener.

그 생각
"that idea (you have)"

그것/그거: This is a **noun** and means "that (thing)." It's used in the same cases as 그.

그거 좋은 생각이에요.
"That is a good idea."

저: This is an **adjective** and means "that." It's used whenever what you're talking about is both far from you — the speaker — and far from the person you're talking with - the listener. You can think of it translating as "that (over there)."

저 사람
"that person (over there)"

저것/저거: This is a **noun** and means "that (thing)" or "that (thing over there)." It's used in the same cases as 저.

저건 뭐죠?
"What is that (thing over there)?"

· · · BONUS EXAMPLES ·

✘ 이것 종이 버려도 돼요?

✓ 이 종이 버려도 돼요?

Meaning "Can I throw away this paper?"

✘ 저것 우산은 누구 거예요?

✓ 저 우산은 누구 거예요?

Meaning "Whose umbrella is that over there?"

This Or That

⊗ **THE WRONG WAY**

이 과자나 저 과자를 먹을까요?

"Should we eat this snack or that snack?"

WHY IS THIS WRONG?

Saying "or" using -(이)나 can't be used when you're asking someone to choose between several options.

⊘ **THE RIGHT WAY**

이 과자 먹을까요?

아니면 저 과자 먹을까요?

"Should we eat this snack or that snack?"

NEVER MAKE THIS MISTAKE AGAIN

There are two distinct ways to say "or" in Korean, depending on how it's being used.

Noun + -(이)나

This form can be used to say "or" when you're making a suggestion to do something. It cannot be used to ask someone to choose between two choices. This is because -(이)나 means "or (something else)." If you were to try asking someone to choose between two options using this form, don't be surprised if they reply with 그래요 ("Sure.").

A: 피자나 햄버거 먹을까요?

"Shall we eat something like pizza or hamburger?"

B: 그래요.

"Sure."

To use this form, take a noun and attach -이나 if it ends in a **consonant**, or attach -나 if it ends in a *vowel*. You can attach another noun after this form — or not (since it's not used for making choices).

이거나 그거
"this thing or that thing"

아니면

This can also be used to say "or" when you're making a suggestion to do something.

피자 아니면 햄버거 먹을까요?
"Should we eat something like pizza or hamburgers?"

However, you can also use this when asking the listener to make a choice. To do this, split the two choices into two separate sentences, using 아니면 at the beginning of the second sentence ("Or…").

피자 먹을까요? 아니면 햄버거 먹을까요?
"Should we eat pizza? Or should we eat hamburgers?"

· · · BONUS EXAMPLES ·

-(이)나	아니면
회의 오늘이나 내일 할까요? "Shall we have a meeting today or tomorrow or something?"	회의 오늘 할까요? 아니면 내일 할까요? "Shall we have our meeting today or tomorrow?"

CHAPTER 52

Well, Excuse Me!

⊗ **THE WRONG WAY**

실례합니다! 저 주문할게요.

"Excuse me! I'll place my order."

⊘ **THE RIGHT WAY**

여기요! 저 주문할게요.

"Excuse me! I'll place my order."

WHY IS THIS WRONG?

실례합니다 is not a common way to say "excuse me" when you want to get someone's attention, nor is it the most common way to say "excuse me" when moving through a crowd. It can sound a bit too formal and unnatural.

NEVER MAKE THIS MISTAKE AGAIN

There are several ways to say "excuse me" in Korean depending on the situation.

실례합니다 This is a formal sounding expression, and is not commonly used in restaurants or in public places when moving past someone. It can also be used at the start of a longer sentence by saying 실례지만 ("Excuse me, but···").

실례지만 누구시죠?

"Excuse me, but who is this?" (on the phone)

잠시만요 This literally means "for just a little bit," and you can use it when trying to make your way through a crowd or past someone. It is a polite expression.

지나가겠습니다 This is a direct phrase that literally means "I'll pass by," and can also be used when trying to move through a crowd. It is a formal expression. It can also be said as 지나갈게요 ("I'll pass by.") in informal situations.

저기요 or 여기요　These phrases literally mean "Over there." and "Over here." respectively, but they're polite and common ways to say "Excuse me." when you want someone's attention (such as when calling out to a waiter in a restaurant). In Korea, you don't need to wait for someone to come to your table at most casual restaurants. Instead, you can call out to them.

Alternatively, if you know who you're calling out to specifically, you can use their *title*. For example, if you know the restaurant's boss, you can say 사장님! ("Boss! Excuse me!") to get their attention.

• • • BONUS EXAMPLES •

Unnatural	Natural	Meaning
실례합니다. 물 좀 더 주세요.	여기요. 물 좀 더 주세요.	"Excuse me. Could I have some more water?"
실례합니다. 메뉴판 좀 갖다주세요.	여기요. 메뉴판 좀 갖다주세요.	"Excuse me. May I see the menu, please?"
실례합니다. 이거 떨어뜨리셨어요.	저기요. 이거 떨어뜨리셨어요.	"Excuse me. You just dropped this."

"Because" Doesn't Mean "Because"

비가 와서 우산(을) 가져가세요.

"It's raining, so bring an umbrella."

"Bring an umbrella because it's raining."

비가 오니까 우산(을) 가져가세요.

"Bring an umbrella because it's raining."

WHY IS THIS WRONG?

The -아/어/여서 ending only means "because" when showing a cause and effect of something. It cannot be used when telling someone to do something, and sounds awkward if used in that way.

NEVER MAKE THIS MISTAKE AGAIN

There are several forms to say "because" in Korean, but each is only used in specific situations.

Verb Stem + -아/어/여서

This form is used to show a **cause and effect** — something happens, and then something else happens as a result. However, the -아/어/여서 form cannot be used when making a command or suggestion. This is because, in those cases, there is no cause and effect being shown.

우리 피곤해서 커피(를) 마시러 가자. ⊗
우리 피곤하니까 커피(를) 마시러 가자. ⊘
"Let's go drink coffee because we're tired."

To use this form, conjugate a verb like normal to the -요 form, and attach -서 (instead of 요). Then finish the rest of the sentence.

배가 아파서 병원에 갔어요.

"I went to the hospital because my stomach hurt."

Verb Stem + -(으)니까

Instead, this form can be used when making a command. However, it cannot be used when expressing some sort of emotion ("I'm happy because⋯" or "I'm sorry because⋯"); for those kind of sentences, use the -아/어/여서 ending.

늦게 오니까 미안해요. ⊗
늦게 와서 미안해요. ⊘
"I'm sorry for coming late."

To use this form, take a verb stem and attach -으니까 if it ends in a **consonant**, or attach -니까 if it ends in a **vowel**. Verb stems ending in ㄹ, ㅂ, or ㅎ will drop those letters first. In addition, verb stems ending in ㅂ will attach 우 before -니까 (becoming 우니까 after the verb stem).

혼자 가면 무서우니까 같이 가요.

"Let's go together because I get scared if I go by myself."

때문에

This is the most standard way of saying "because," and is also **formal**. However, this form (like the -(으)니까 form) cannot be used when making a command.

비가 오고 있기 때문에 우산을 가져가세요. ⊗

"Bring an umbrella because it is raining."

It's Because Of You!

(×) **THE WRONG WAY**

아빠 때문에 한국으로 이사 갈 수 있었어요.

"I could move to Korea because of you, Dad."

(✓) **THE RIGHT WAY**

아빠 덕분에 한국으로 이사 갈 수 있었어요.

"I could move to Korea thanks to you, Dad."

WHY IS THIS WRONG?

Saying "because" using the **때문에** form implies that someone *caused* something, but not in a good way. It tends to be used with a person to say that someone did something *negative* (bad). Here, since the sentence starts with **아빠 때문에**, it sounds like you are going to *blame* your father for something instead of thanking him. However, the next part of the sentence is **이사 갈 수 있었어요**, which would be something considered positive, so the sentence doesn't sound natural.

NEVER MAKE THIS MISTAKE AGAIN

In English, we can say "because of" someone when we want to thank them or owe some accomplishment to that person. For example, you could say "I won because of you" when you are thanking someone.

형 때문에 제가 이겼어요. (×)
"I won because of you, brother."

However, using 때문에 to *thank* someone sounds awkward — even if the sentence's meaning is innocent. It will sound like you are *blaming* someone, so it shouldn't be used after a person.

Instead, to thank a person, use 덕분에 ("thanks to") in the middle of a sentence, or 덕분이다 at the end of a sentence.

제 친구 덕분에 한국어를 배울 수 있었어요.
"I could learn Korean thanks to my friend."

다 선생님 덕분입니다.
"It's all thanks to you, Teacher."

· · · **BONUS EXAMPLES** ·

ⓧ 경화 씨 때문에 싸게 샀어요.

✓ 경화 씨 덕분에 싸게 샀어요.

Meaning "Thanks to Kyung-hwa, I got it cheap."

ⓧ 석진 씨 때문에 TV 출연했어요.

✓ 석진 씨 덕분에 TV 출연했어요.

Meaning "Thanks to Seokjin, I appeared on TV."

ⓧ TTMIK 때문에 제 한국어가 늘었어요.

✓ TTMIK 덕분에 제 한국어가 늘었어요.

Meaning "Thanks to TTMIK, my Korean has improved."

Again And Again

⊗ THE WRONG WAY

다시 감사합니다.

"Thank you again."

⊘ THE RIGHT WAY

다시 한번 감사합니다.

"Thank you again."

WHY IS THIS WRONG?

Using 다시 ("again") shows that you're doing something anew or repeating something again that you've done before. However, when you're thanking someone "again," you mean to emphasize that you're really thankful, and not that you're simply saying "thank you" a second time, so this sentence sounds awkward.

NEVER MAKE THIS MISTAKE AGAIN

다시 한번 means "once again" or "for a second time," and can be used when repeating some expression for emphasis. Although saying 다시 한번 감사합니다 is correct and means "Thank you again," it sounds formal and is less common. Instead, to thank someone for something, there's usually no need to say "again" — simply say "thank you" a second time.

Not only can 다시 be incorrectly used, but also can 또 be for the same reason. 다시 and 또 both mean "again," but are used in different situations.

다시 This means "again," and is used when you're repeating something (doing something again) — perhaps in the same way as you've done it before or in an entirely new way. This means that you're doing something not only again, but *anew*. For example, you might need to make a cake again if you messed up the first time and are going to start from the very beginning — 다시 만들 거예요 ("I'll make it again.").

다시 생각해 볼게요.

"I'll think about it again (from the start)."

또   This means "again," and is also used when you're repeating something. In addition, it can also have a slightly negative connotation to it, but this depends on how it's being used. For example, you might use 또 if your mother asks you to clean the bathroom again — 또 해야 돼? ("I have to do it again?").

계획이 또 실패했어.

"The plan failed again."

또 그 드라마 보고 있어요?

"Are you watching the drama again?"

Another important difference between 다시 and 또 is that 또 can also have the meaning of "additionally," whereas 다시 cannot. For example, you could say 또 주세요 to mean "Please give me more." But the same sentence with 다시 would sound like you were saying "Please take this back, and give it to me again," such as what an adult might say when scolding a child and asking them to do something again more politely.

⋯ BONUS EXAMPLES ⋯

⊗ 다시 축하드립니다.

✓ 다시 한번 축하드립니다.

Meaning "Congratulations again."

⊗ 다시 죄송합니다.

✓ 다시 한번 죄송합니다.

Meaning "I am sorry again."

⊗ 다시 사과드립니다.

✓ 다시 한번 사과드립니다.

Meaning "I apologize again."

Setting The Topic

⊗ **THE WRONG WAY**

저는 미국 사람이에요.
저는 엘에이에서 왔어요.
저는 한국어를 공부하고 있어요.

"I'm American. I'm from LA.
I'm studying Korean."

⊘ **THE RIGHT WAY**

저는 미국 사람이에요.
엘에이에서 왔어요.
한국어를 공부하고 있어요.

"I'm American. I'm from LA.
I'm studying Korean."

WHY IS THIS WRONG?

The Topic Marker, -은/는, does not need to be repeated once the topic has been set.
Starting every sentence with **저는** sounds repetitive and strange, like saying "As for
me, I'm American. As for me, I'm from LA. As for me, I'm studying Korean."

NEVER MAKE THIS MISTAKE AGAIN

The topic marker, -은/는, is often misused or overused due to a misunderstanding of
its usage.

-은/는: To use the topic marker, attach -은 after a **_consonant_**, or attach -는 after a
vowel.

The topic marker is used just like its name says — to mark the **_topic_** of whatever
you're talking about. That means that once the topic is marked (once), there's no
need to repeatedly mark it again unless the topic is changing.

One way to think of the topic marker is to imagine a sign hanging above your head
at all times. Written on that sign is the current topic of the conversation or the
sentence you're saying. Whenever someone uses the topic marker, replace what's
written on the sign with the new topic. There's no need to use another topic marker

unless you're changing the topic of the sentence.

김밥은 맛있어요. 그리고 싸요.
"Kimbap tastes good (the "topic" sign now says 김밥). And it (김밥) is cheap."

Another way to think of the topic marker is to translate it as "As for…" or "When it comes to…." Think of 저는 as translating to "As for me…," and you won't want to use it more than is necessary. Using these terms can be useful because they also show in English that you're changing the topic of what you're talking about.

저는 한국어를 열심히 공부하고 있어요. 한국을 정말 좋아해요!
"As for me, I'm studying Korean hard. I really like Korea!"

Unnatural	Natural	Meaning
저는 제니퍼입니다. 저는 열여덟 살이고 저는 대학생입니다.	저는 제니퍼입니다. 열여덟 살이고 대학생입니다.	"I'm Jennifer. I'm 18, and I'm a college student."
이 영화는 한국에서 인기가 많아요. 이 영화는 미국에서는 인기가 없대요.	이 영화는 한국에서 인기가 많아요. 미국에서는 인기가 없대요.	"This movie is popular in Korea. They say that it's not popular in the States."
밤은 위장에 좋대요. 밤은 피부에도 좋대요.	밤은 위장에 좋대요. 피부에도 좋대요.	"It is said that chestnuts are good for the stomach. They are also said to be good for the skin."

CHAPTER 57

Choosing The Topic

⊗ **THE WRONG WAY**

저는 그 영화는 재미있어요.

"To me, that movie is fun."

⊘ **THE RIGHT WAY**

저는 그 영화(가) 재미있어요.

"To me, that movie is fun."

WHY IS THIS WRONG?

It's not necessary to change the topic mid-sentence with the topic marker, -은/는. In the example, the topic is already set as **저** ("I," "me"), so it would be better to mark **영화** ("movie") with something else to describe it. Using two topic markers usually sounds repetitive and odd.

NEVER MAKE THIS MISTAKE AGAIN

Instead of using the topic marker, -은/는, more than once in a sentence, Koreans tend to omit the second marker (mostly done in spoken language) or use the subject marker instead (mostly done in written language). The subject marker just marks the subject of a verb, and does not set the topic of a conversation.

저는 그 영화 재미있어요. (spoken style)
저는 그 영화가 재미있어요. (written style)

However, there are cases where you can find two topic markers in one sentence, and that's when you're comparing two or more things. For example, if you're comparing two or more movies, you could say 저는 그 영화'는' 재미있어요. In this case, the emphasis of the sentence moves to "그 영화는 (= as for that movie)" rather than "저는 (= to me)." When doing this, put more emphasis on the -는 in 그 영화는 to make it clear that you're implying "That movie is at least fun to me."

Here's another example:

저는 인터넷으로는 컴퓨터를 샀어요.
저는 인터넷으로 컴퓨터를 샀어요.
"I bought a computer online."

If you were trying to simply say "As for me, I bought a computer online," then only the second sentence would sound natural. The first sentence would only sound natural if you were comparing buying a computer online with other places (such as offline). In this way, you could use two topic markers to mean something like this: "As for online, I bought a computer, and as for offline, I bought some clothes."

BONUS EXAMPLES

Unnatural	Natural	Meaning
이 가수는 한국에서는 인기가 없대요. * It can sound natural if you are comparing Korea with another country.	이 가수는 한국에서 인기가 없대요. 이 가수 한국에서는 인기가 없대요. 이 가수가 한국에서는 인기가 없대요.	"I heard that this singer is not popular in Korea."
사과는 밤에 먹는 것은 안 좋대요. * It can sound natural if you are comparing eating at night with eating at another time.	사과는 밤에 먹는 것이 안 좋대요. 사과는 밤에 먹으면 안 좋대요. 사과를 밤에 먹는 것은 안 좋대요.	"They say that eating apples at night is not good."

Don't Overuse The Object Marker

⊗ **THE WRONG WAY**

저는 한국어를 공부를 하고 싶어요.

"I want to study Korean."

⊘ **THE RIGHT WAY**

저는 한국어를 공부하고 싶어요.

"I want to study Korean."

WHY IS THIS WRONG?

Grammatically, the object marker, -을/를, is used to mark the object of an action verb — what that verb is doing something to. The object marker can also optionally be used between Sino-Korean verbs that use 하다. However, using both so close together can sound repetitive and, therefore, unnatural.

NEVER MAKE THIS MISTAKE AGAIN

There are many action verbs that end in -하다, and Koreans often attach the object marker, -을/를, between them. For example, Koreans will often use 공부를 하다 instead of 공부하다 and 청소를 하다 instead of 청소하다, especially when spoken.

However, if a sentence already contains an object (with the object marker attached to it), it's better not to repeat the object marker again to sound more natural.

Ex)
방을 청소를 하고 있어요. ⊗
방을 청소하고 있어요. ⊘
"I am cleaning up the room."

In fact, you can also omit the first object marker here, and instead, attach it between the action verb (before -하다).

저는 한국어를 공부를 하고 싶어요. ⊗
저는 한국어를 공부하고 싶어요. ⊘
저는 한국어 공부를 하고 싶어요. ⊘

방을 청소를 하고 있어요. ⊗
방을 청소하고 있어요. ⊘
방 청소를 하고 있어요. ⊘

• • • • BONUS EXAMPLES •

⊗ 그 사람을 사랑을 해요?

⊘ 그 사람을 사랑해요?

Meaning   "Do you love him/her?"

⊗ 친구를 용서를 했어요.

⊘ 친구를 용서했어요.

Meaning   "I forgave my friend."

⊗ 제가 주연 씨 이름을 기억을 했어요.

⊘ 제가 주연 씨 이름을 기억했어요.

Meaning   "I remembered Jooyeon's name."

131

How Not To Combine Particles

⊗ **THE WRONG WAY**

저도에게 말해 주세요.

"Please tell me too."

WHY IS THIS WRONG?

Certain particles can only combine in specific ways, such as -**에게** and -**도** — these can only combine to form -**에게도**. While every particle works differently, some have strict rules, and breaking those rules can make the whole sentence sound unnatural. This sentence would therefore translate like, "Please tell too to me."

⊘ **THE RIGHT WAY**

저에게도 말해 주세요.

저한테도 말해 주세요.

"Please tell me too."

NEVER MAKE THIS MISTAKE AGAIN

Each Korean particle has its own rules for how to use it, and also how it can be combined with other particles. Some can replace others entirely, or prefer to come before or after others. Here are some of the most common combinations for the topic marker, -은/는, subject marker, -이/가, object marker, -을/를, as well as the particles -도, -만, and -에게.

-은/는 + -이/가: These cannot be combined. Choose only one or the other. Unless you need to emphasize the subject of a verb (such as when answering a question about "who" did something), use 은/는 instead.

저는가 ⊗
제가 or 저는
"I…"

-은/는 + -도: These cannot be combined. Instead, use only 도.

저는도 ⊗
저도는 ⊗
저도 ✓
"I also…"

-은/는 + -에게: This becomes -에게는. Also, -한테 will become -한테는.

저는에게 ⊗
저에게는 ✓
"To me…"

-이/가 + -도: These cannot be combined. Instead, use only 도.

내가도 ⊗
나도가 ⊗
나도 ✓
"I also…"

-을/를 + -도: These cannot be combined. Instead, use only 도.

그것을도 ⊗
그것도 ✓
"That (thing) too…"

-을/를 + -만: This becomes -만을 (more formal) or -만 (more casual).

그 사람을만 좋아해요. ⊗
그 사람만(을) 좋아해요. ✓
"I only like that person."

Adding Emotion

⊗ **THE WRONG WAY**

와! 생각보다 맛있어요.

누가 맛없다고 했어요?

저 집에 좀 가져가도 돼요?

"Wow! It tastes better than I thought.
Who said it doesn't taste good?
Can I take some home?"

⊘ **THE RIGHT WAY**

와! 생각보다 맛있네요!

누가 맛없다고 했어요?

저 집에 좀 가져가도 되나요?

와! 생각보다 맛있는데요?

누가 맛없다고 했어요?

저 집에 좀 가져가도 되죠?

"Wow! It tastes better than I thought!
Who said it doesn't taste good?
Can I take some home, right?"

WHY IS THIS WRONG?

These sentences are grammatically correct, but none of them really show any emotion because they are using the basic sentence endings only. These sentences would translate correctly in English, but in Korean, would sound boring and flat.

NEVER MAKE THIS MISTAKE AGAIN

In English, we can add intonation or extra words to our sentences in order to show our emotions. In Korean, you can add these sort of emotions to your sentence by simply changing the verb ending.

To use all of these verb endings, attach them directly to a verb stem.

-네(요) or -(으/느)ㄴ데(요)? These endings add a feeling of *surprise* to your sentence.

Ex)

제가 아는 사람이 아무도 없네요. or 제가 아는 사람이 아무도 없는데요?

"Wow, there's nobody who I know."

둘이 정말 닮았네요. or 둘이 정말 닮았는데요?

"Wow, you two really look alike."

-나(요)? This ending makes a question sound softer. Therefore, it's often used when asking for something.

저도 갈 수 있나요?

"Can I go too?"

여기 앉으면 되나요?

"Should I sit down here?"

-지(요)? This ending shows that you want the other person to **_confirm_** what you're saying. Therefore, it can translate to "isn't it?" or "right?" or even "huh?" or "eh?"

제가 만들었어요. 잘했죠?

"I made it. I did a good job, huh?"

이 코트 입어도 되죠?

"I can wear this coat, right?"

· · BONUS EXAMPLES ·

Flat	Expressive	Meaning
생각보다 깨끗해요.	생각보다 깨끗하네요!	"Wow, it's cleaner than I thought!"

135

DIAGNOSE WHAT'S WRONG WITH THIS SENTENCE.

오 달 동안 여행했어요.

See Chapter 66

Adding More Emotion

⊗ **THE WRONG WAY**

경화: 저는 보라색을 제일 좋아해요.

"I like purple the most."

경은: 아, 경화 씨는 보라색을 제일
좋아해요.

"Ah, you like purple the most."

⊘ **THE RIGHT WAY**

경화: 저는 보라색을 제일 좋아해요.

"I like purple the most."

경은: 아, 경화 씨는 보라색을 제일
좋아하는군요.

"Ah, I see you like purple the most."

WHY IS THIS WRONG?

If you were to reply with **경화 씨는 보라색을 제일 좋아해요**, it would sound like you're simply repeating a piece of information — "You like purple the most." One way to avoid this would be to ask it as a question: **아, 경화 씨는 보라색을 제일 좋아해요?** ("Ah, do you like purple the most?"). However, just repeating information back to someone shows no extra emotion, and the listener might wonder why you are stating something that is obvious. Instead, it would sound much more natural to add some emotion to show the listener that you've only just *realized* they like the color purple most, and are repeating it for that reason.

NEVER MAKE THIS MISTAKE AGAIN

-(는)군요 This ending adds a feeling of *realizing something* to your sentence. For example, if you've just noticed that someone already left, you might want to say "Oh!" or "So..." or another similar expression to show that you've just realized that fact. To use this ending, attach it directly to the verb stem. Note that action verb stems in the *present tense* will use -는군요; and action verb stems ending in ㄹ will remove the ㄹ before adding -는군요. For other tenses (such as the past tense), simply attach -군요 to the verb stem for both descriptive verbs and action verbs.

지금 나가는군요.
"Oh, he's leaving now."

미국 사람이시군요!
"So you're an American!"

김치를 좋아하는군요.
"Oh, he likes kimchi."

이미 나갔군요.
"Oh, he already left."

Note that -(는)구나 is another version of -(는)군요 that has the same meaning, but can only be used in **casual speech**. When used with action verbs in the present tense, attach -는구나; action verb stems ending in ㄹ will remove the ㄹ before adding -는구나.

정말 맛있군요!
정말 맛있구나!
"Oh, it's really good!"

김치를 진짜 좋아하는군요.
김치를 진짜 좋아하는구나.
"Wow, he really likes kimchi."

·· BONUS EXAMPLES ·····························

When you have just realized:

✗ 아! 예지 씨는 가까운 곳에 살아요.

✓ 아! 예지 씨는 가까운 곳에 사는군요.

> Meaning

"(To Yeji) Oh, you live close!"

✗ 주연 씨는 밀가루 음식을 싫어해요.

✓ 주연 씨는 밀가루 음식을 싫어하는군요.

> Meaning

"(To Jooyeon) I see you don't like flour-based foods!"

139

CHAPTER 62

You Can't Play A Computer

⊗ **THE WRONG WAY**

컴퓨터 게임(을) 놀고 싶어요?

"Do you want to play computer games?"

⊘ **THE RIGHT WAY**

컴퓨터 게임(을) 하고 싶어요?

"Do you want to play computer games?"

WHY IS THIS WRONG?

놀다 means "to play," but it's not the correct verb to use when you are playing **something**. Instead, 놀다 means "to play" as in "to play with others" or "to hang out with others." This sentence would, therefore, sound like "Do you want to hang out a computer game?"

NEVER MAKE THIS MISTAKE AGAIN

There are various words for "to play" depending on what you are playing. Here are the most common and useful ones:

하다 This means "to do," and it can be used whenever you're playing a **game** or an **activity**.

이 게임을 한 시간 동안 했어요.
"I played this game for one hour."

켜다 This means "to bow," and it can be used whenever you're playing a **bow instrument** — such as a violin.

친구가 바이올린을 잘 켜요.
"My friend plays the violin well."

치다 This means "to hit," and it can be used whenever you're playing a **string instrument** — such as a guitar or a piano (which has strings on the inside). Note that string instruments played with a bow will still use 켜다.

피아노를 칠 줄 아세요?
"Do you know how to play the piano?"

불다 This means "to blow," and it can be used whenever you're playing any instrument that can be **blown into** — such as the clarinet, the flute, or the trumpet. This includes both wind instruments and brass instruments.

저는 뱀 옆에서 피리를 불었어요.
"I played a pipe next to a snake."

연주하다 This means "to play," and it can be used with **any instrument**. However, this verb sounds a little bit **formal** (almost like saying "to perform"), so it's best to use one of the other verbs instead if you're able to.

친구들과 함께 기타 연주를 했어요.
"I played the guitar together with friends."

· · BONUS EXAMPLES ·

⊗ 저는 일요일마다 축구 놀아요.

✓ 저는 일요일마다 축구 해요.

> Meaning "I play soccer every Sunday."

⊗ 피아노 놀 줄 몰라요.

✓ 피아노 칠 줄 몰라요.

> Meaning "I don't know how to play the piano."

CHAPTER 63

The Third Person

⊗ **THE WRONG WAY**

철수도 공원으로 가고 싶어요.

"Chul-soo also wants to go to the park."

⊘ **THE RIGHT WAY**

철수도 공원으로 가고 싶어해요.

"Chul-soo also wants to go to the park."

WHY IS THIS WRONG?

Using 가고 싶어요 about another person — a third person — is unnatural and grammatically incorrect. This is because using this form means that you're 100% sure what someone wants, and in Korean, that's not possible to know.

NEVER MAKE THIS MISTAKE AGAIN

In English, there are three ways to speak about something — using the first person, the second person, and the third person. These terms sound more complicated than they are. The ***first person*** means that you're talking about yourself; you can say "I want to go." The ***second person*** means that you're talking about the person you're talking about; "You want to go." The ***third person*** means that you're talking about someone else — not yourself or the person you're talking with. In this case, you can say "He/she wants to go" or "Billy wants to go."

In English, it's okay to use the same grammar ("to want to go") with all three cases. In Korean, whenever you're talking directly about another person's emotions or desires (wants), you'll need to use a different form when speaking using the ***third person***. This is because it's assumed that you can't know for certain what a third person feels or wants.

저는 삼겹살 먹고 싶어요. ⊘

"I want to eat pork belly."

너 삼겹살 먹고 싶어? ⊘ (casual)
"Do you want to eat pork belly?"

그 사람은 삼겹살 먹고 싶어요. ⊗
"That person wants to eat pork belly."

Normally, a person's emotions and desires can be described using *descriptive verbs*, but you'll need to change that descriptive verb into an *action verb* to use it correctly in the third person.

Descriptive Verb Stem + -아/어/여하다

To use this form, take a descriptive verb (another person's emotions or desires), and conjugate it to the 요 form, removing the 요. Then attach 하다 and conjugate it.

슬프다 → 슬퍼하다
그립다 → 그리워하다
기쁘다 → 기뻐하다
가지고 싶다 → 가지고 싶어하다

저는 갈래요. 현우 씨도 갈래요. ⊗
저는 갈래요. 현우 씨도 가고 싶어해요. ⊘
"I want to go. Hyunwoo wants to go too."

마이크 씨도 한국 음식을 먹어 보고 싶어. ⊗
마이크 씨도 한국 음식을 먹어 보고 싶어해요. ⊘
"Mike also wants to try Korean food."

There is an exception to this. If you are 100% certain about a third person's emotions or desires, then it's fine to not use this form. This could happen if you're the writer of a book who's describing your characters.

CHAPTER 64

Don't Be Sad

⊗ **THE WRONG WAY**

슬프지 마세요.

"Don't be sad."

⊘ **THE RIGHT WAY**

슬퍼하지 마세요.

"Don't be sad."

WHY IS THIS WRONG?

슬프다 means "to be sad," so it's understandable that someone might try to say "Don't be sad" by using the **-지 마세요** ending ("Please don't⋯"). However, this ending is only for *action verbs*, and this is not a natural way to tell someone not to be a *descriptive verb*.

NEVER MAKE THIS MISTAKE AGAIN

It's grammatically incorrect to command someone using a descriptive verb. For example, it would be incorrect to say "Don't be afraid" by simply using the descriptive verb 무섭다 ("to be scared") as 무섭지 마세요. In order to change a *descriptive verb* into a command — such as "do" or "don't" — you first need to change into an *action verb*.

Descriptive Verb Stem + -아/어/여하다

Just as we learned before, to change a descriptive verb to an action verb, first conjugate it to the 요 form (minus the 요), and then attach 하다.

무서워하지 마세요.

"Don't be afraid."

This form can create simple commands — "do" and "don't" — but it's limited in how it will be used in natural Korean.

Adverb + 굴지 말다

To tell someone "not" to **act** or ***behave***, take an adverb and attach 굴지 말다, then conjugate it (such as to 굴지 마세요). 굴다 means "to act" or "to behave."

무례하게 굴지 마세요.
"Don't be rude."

못되게 굴지 마요.
"Don't be mean."

이상하게 굴지 마세요.
"Don't be weird."

There are a few exceptions. The verbs 행복하다 ("to be happy"), 건강하다 ("to be healthy"), and 아프다 ("to be sick") are often used directly as commands, so much that they're considered to be correct phrases.

행복하세요!
"Be happy!"

건강하세요!
"Be healthy!"

아프지 마세요!
"Don't be sick!"

···· **BONUS EXAMPLES** ···

✗ 고마우세요.

✓ 고마워하세요.

Meaning   "Be thankful for it."

⊗ **THE WRONG WAY**

오늘 너무 더워요. 구십오예요!

"Today's so hot. It's 95!"

⊘ **THE RIGHT WAY**

너무 더워요. 삼십오 도예요!

"Today's so hot. It's 35 degrees!"

WHY IS THIS WRONG?

Korean temperature is said using Celsius. In addition, temperature is counted with a *counter* — just like everything else is counted. This sentence would sound like you're saying, "It's 95 degrees Celsius (all life is dead)" or randomly shouting the number "95" for no reason.

NEVER MAKE THIS MISTAKE AGAIN

If you want to be specific when telling someone the weather, you can use a *counter*. Korean temperature is counted with the *counter* 도.

도 This counter means "degrees," and is used together with Sino-Korean numbers.

이십 도
"20 degrees"

영 도
"zero degrees"

현재 체온은 삼십칠 도입니다.
"The body's temperature is 37 degrees at the moment."

If you want to specify "below" or "above," use 이하 ("below") and 이상 ("above").

오늘도 기온이 사십 도 이상일 거예요.
"Today's temperature will also be above 40 degrees."

In addition, Korea uses Celsius (not Fahrenheit like the United States). If you're not familiar with Celsius, searching online when converting the exact temperature is recommended. For a quick reference, you can remember this rhyme:

Thirty's hot and twenty's nice.
Ten is cold and zero's ice.

To ask the temperature (in degrees), use 몇 before 도. This literally means "how many degrees."

오늘은 몇 도예요?
"How many degrees is it today?"
"What's the temperature today?"

· · · BONUS EXAMPLES ·

⊗ 오늘 최고 기온 삼십육이에요.

✓ 오늘 최고 기온 삼십육 도예요.

Meaning · "Today the high is 36 degrees."

⊗ 오늘 영하 칠이래요.

✓ 오늘 영하 칠 도래요.

Meaning · "Apparently, it's -7 degrees today."

⊗ 내일 영하 십까지 내려간대요.

✓ 내일 영하 십 도까지 내려간대요.

Meaning · "It's said that the temperature will drop to -10 degrees tomorrow."

Counting Months

⊗ **THE WRONG WAY**

저는 삼 달 동안 공부했어요.

"I studied for three months."

✓ **THE RIGHT WAY**

저는 세 달 동안 공부했어요.

"I studied for three months."

WHY IS THIS WRONG?

달 ("month") is a counter only used with pure Korean numbers. While **삼 달** would make sense to someone who is listening intently, it sounds awkward and incorrect because it's using the wrong number system.

NEVER MAKE THIS MISTAKE AGAIN

Previously, we learned about how to count days using Sino-Korean numbers and 일 and how to count years with 년. Counters are a frequently misused concept in Korean due to how many there are and how some of them can seem similar to others. There are three counters you need to know when counting months:

달 This counter can be used to count "months," and is used together with pure Korean numbers.

두 달
"two months"

여섯 달
"six months"

개월 This counter can also be used to count "months," but is used together with Sino-Korean numbers.
육 개월

"six months"

이십삼 개월
"23 months"

Feel free to use either 달 or 개월, but remember to use the correct number system with each.

오 달 동안 여행했어요. ⊗
다섯 개월 동안 여행했어요. ⊗
오 개월 동안 여행했어요. ⊘
다섯 달 동안 여행했어요. ⊘
"I traveled for five months"

To simply say what month it is, use the counter 월 ("month") together with Sino-Korean numbers. Here are all 12 months of the year. Note the unique spellings (and pronunciation) for the months of June and October:

일월 January
이월 February
삼월 March
사월 April
오월 May
유월 June
칠월 July
팔월 August
구월 September
시월 October
십일월 November
십이월 December

CHAPTER 67

Inside Or Within

⊗ **THE WRONG WAY**

두 시간 안에 보자!

"See you in two hours!"

⊘ **THE RIGHT WAY**

두 시간 후에 보자!

"See you in two hours!"

WHY IS THIS WRONG?

안 means "inside," but has a different meaning when used together with *time*. In this sentence, it sounds like you intend to see the other person *before* two hours has elapsed — not *after*.

NEVER MAKE THIS MISTAKE AGAIN

안 ("inside") is normally used to show that something is *physically* inside of something. For example, your car keys might be inside of a box.

차 키가 상자 안에 있어요.

"The car keys are in the box."

안에 In English, we can say "in" with an amount of time to mean "after" that amount of time has elapsed. In Korean, it works differently. When used with *time*, 안 means "within" — before an amount of time has elapsed. Saying 2시간 안에 means "in *less than* two hours" and not "after."

3일 안에 할 거예요.

"I'll do it within three days."

전에 This means "ago" or "before." It is useful when you want to emphasize that something happens *before* a specified time.

한 시간 전에 만났어요.
"I met him an hour ago."

후에   This means "after," and is a better way to translate "in" when referring to time.

현우 씨는 30분 후에 올 것 같아요.
"I think Hyunwoo will come in 30 minutes."

-까지   This means either "until" or "by," depending on the context. If you wanted to say that something should happen **before**, but **no later than** another time, you could use this. For example, if you're working on a project and the deadline is next week, then you have **until** next week to finish it (or it must be finished **by** next week).

다음 주까지 다 끝내야 돼요.
"I have to finish it all by next week."

· · · BONUS EXAMPLES ·

안에	후에
세 시간 안에 드세요. "Please eat it within three hours."	세 시간 후에 드세요. "Please eat it in three hours."
한 시간 안에 나가야 돼요. "I have to go out within an hour."	한 시간 후에 나가야 돼요. "I have to go out in an hour."
3일 안에 도착할 거예요. "It will arrive within three days."	3일 후에 도착할 거예요. "It will arrive in three days."

Family Terms

저는 마이크의 오빠한테 물어봤어요.

"I asked Mike's older brother."

저는 마이크의 형한테 물어봤어요.

"I asked Mike's older brother."

WHY IS THIS WRONG?

Family terms, such as 오빠 ("older brother"), are unique depending on who's using them and whom they're in reference to. In the example, saying 오빠 to mean "older brother" would be incorrect even if you are a female because 오빠 is being used in reference to Mike. This sentence would sound like Mike is a female instead.

NEVER MAKE THIS MISTAKE AGAIN

There are two ways to use family terms, such as 오빠, 언니, 형, and 누나.

When talking about **yourself** — your 오빠, 언니, 형, and 누나 — you only need to choose the correct term depending on your gender.

Males use the terms 형 ("older brother") and 누나 ("older sister"). Females use the terms 오빠 ("older brother") and 언니 ("older sister").

Here's where it gets a bit more complicated. When talking about **someone else**, you need to choose the correct term depending on that person's gender — regardless of your own gender. This means you should refer to a female friend's "older brother" as 오빠 and her "older sister" as 언니. You should also refer to a male friend's "older brother" as 형 and his "older sister" as 누나.

Note that this only applies when talking about that other person with the male or female friend, and not when directly talking to the family member. For example, if you're a male, then you still should use 형 when talking to a female friend's "older brother," but you should call that "older brother" 오빠 when mentioning him to that female friend (if you met him and called him 오빠, it would sound like you were imitating a female).

(Boy to Girl)
형한테 물어봤어? ⊗
오빠한테 물어봤어? ⊘
"Did you ask your older brother?"

(Girl to Boy)
언니는 뭐 해요? ⊗
누나는 뭐 해요? ⊘
"What does your older sister do?"

Note that both males and females can use 동생 ("younger sibling"), 남동생 ("younger male sibling"), or 여동생 ("younger female sibling").

• • • BONUS EXAMPLES •

⊗ 형이 도와줬어요?

⊘ 오빠가 도와줬어요?

Meaning "(Boy to Girl) "Did your older brother help you?"

⊗ 언니랑 같이 갔다 왔어요?

⊘ 누나랑 같이 갔다 왔어요?

Meaning "(Girl to Boy) "Have you been there with your older sister?"

⊗ 누나랑 많이 닮았네요.

⊘ 언니랑 많이 닮았네요.

Meaning "(Boy to Girl) "You really look like your older sister."

How To Make Friends

⊗ THE WRONG WAY

저는 선생님의 친구예요.

"I'm friends with the teacher."

⊘ THE RIGHT WAY

저는 선생님하고 친해요.

"I'm friends with the teacher."

WHY IS THIS WRONG?

The word 친구 isn't thrown around as easily in Korean as it is in English. Although you can be friends with anyone, 친구 isn't used with people who are much older than you. Calling a teacher 친구 could sound a bit insulting.

NEVER MAKE THIS MISTAKE AGAIN

The word 친구 ("friend") is used with people who are both close to you (just like "friend" in English), but only with people who are also the same Korean age as you. This is related to Korean culture, where a person's age can determine the way that you speak to them, and people typically spend their free time around others who are a similar age as them.

Therefore, for someone you are close with who's much older than you, it would be preferable to simply say that they're someone *close* to or friendly with you than to call them 친구. This depends on a case by case basis, but it's better to be careful than impolite.

저는 사장님하고 친해요.

"I'm close with the boss."

Alternatively, you can also refer to someone who is close with you using **친한** before their title, which literally means "close."

친한 선생님
"close teacher"

Or you can use **친하게 지내는** before their title (like an adjective), which literally means "whom I'm close with."

친하게 지내는 선생님
"teacher whom I'm close with"

If you are even closer with them, you can also use kinship terms such as 오빠, 언니, 형, and 누나. In this case, it's not necessary for them to be directly related to you or in your family.

친한 언니
"female friend whom is older than me"

친한 누나
"female friend whom is older than me"

These days, as more Koreans are being affected by western culture, there are some people who will refer to each other using 친구 even though they are not the same age. However, this is still less common, and most Koreans will tend to use different expressions in these cases, such as **친구처럼 지내다** (literally, "to get along together like friends").

저희는 친구처럼 지내요.
"We get along together like friends."

If you were to say this, it wouldn't only mean that you were close with someone, but also that the older friend has allowed the younger friend to speak with them using casual language in order to be more comfortable.

Suggestions Can Be Rude

⊗ **THE WRONG WAY**

팀장님, 산책할래요?

"Chief, do you want to take a walk?"

⊙ **THE RIGHT WAY**

팀장님, 산책하실래요?

"Chief, do you want to take a walk?"

WHY IS THIS WRONG?

The -(으)ㄹ래요 ending means "want to," and is an informal grammar form (even though it ends with -요), which can translate as "wanna." This can sound too casual (and therefore impolite) when speaking with an older person at a formal setting.

NEVER MAKE THIS MISTAKE AGAIN

There are several ways to make suggestions in Korean, depending on the amount of politeness and the meaning of the sentence. In English, we can make suggestions by asking someone if they want to do something ("Do you want to···") or by asking with "shall" ("Shall we···"). Here are those two forms in Korean:

Action Verb Stem + -(으)ㄹ래요?

This is a direct way to ask someone if they want to (or "wanna") do something. However, speaking directly in Korean, especially to someone older, can also be seen as impolite.

To use this form, take an action verb stem and attach -을래요 if it ends in a **consonant**, or attach -ㄹ래요 if it ends in a **vowel**.

한국어 같이 공부할래요?

"Do you want to study Korean together?"

영화 보러 갈래요?

"Do you want to see a movie?"

In order to make it sound politer, you need to attach the honorific suffix -시- to -(으)ㄹ래요? and say -(으)실래요? unless the older person you are suggesting is one of your close acquaintances whom you can call 오빠/언니/형/누나.

Action Verb Stem + -(으)ㄹ까요?

In English, "Shall we⋯" isn't such a commonly used way of making a suggestion, but it is in Korean. In fact, using "Shall we" instead of "Want to" is a more polite way of making a suggestion (such as when suggesting something to someone older or someone who isn't a close friend or acquaintance).

To use this form, take an action verb stem and attach -을까요 if it ends in a **consonant**, or attach -ㄹ까요 if it ends in a **vowel**.

이거 두 개 살까요?

"Shall we buy two of these?"

추우면 창문 닫을까요?

"If you're cold, should we close the window?"

저부터 할까요?

"Shall we do it starting from me?"

"Shall I go first?"

· · BONUS EXAMPLES ·

Inappropriate/Impolite	Appropriate/Polite	Meaning
제 것 쓸래요?	제 것 쓰실래요?	"Do you want to use mine?"

The 데 Form

저는 김치를 별로 안 좋아한데.

"I don't like kimchi much."

저는 김치를 별로 안 좋아하는데…

"I don't like kimchi much."

WHY IS THIS WRONG?

When using the 데 form (in this case, **좋아한데**), the type of verb — action or descriptive — affects the conjugation. When conjugated incorrectly, it will sound unnatural.

NEVER MAKE THIS MISTAKE AGAIN

The 데 form is useful for these two purposes: to **contrast** two sentences and to **explain** something. This lesson won't cover how to use the 데 form in detail, but only how it's often misused.

Contrast: 저는 김치를 안 좋아하는데 만들 수는 있어요.
"I don't like kimchi, but I can make it."

Explaining: 김치를 안 좋아하는데…
"(So you see…) I don't like kimchi."

The 데 form conjugates slightly differently depending on whether the verb it's attached to is an **action verb** or a **descriptive verb**.

Action Verb Stem + -는데

For action verbs in the **present tense**, take the verb stem and attach -는데.

가다 → 가는데
먹다 → 먹는데
좋아하다 → 좋아하는데

Descriptive Verb Stem + -(으)ㄴ데

For descriptive verbs in the **present tense**, take the verb stem and attach -은데 if it ends in a **consonant**, or attach -ㄴ데 if it ends in a **vowel**. Verb stems ending in ㄹ, ㅂ, or ㅎ will drop those letters first. In addition, verb stems ending in ㅂ will attach 우 before ㄴ데 (becoming 운데 after the verb stem).

덥다 → 더운데
멀다 → 먼데
좋다 → 좋은데

One exception is the descriptive verb 있다, which becomes 있는데 (and not 있은데).

For both action verbs and descriptive verbs in the **past tense**, conjugate the verb and attach -는데 to the conjugated stem.

가다
Past: 갔다 → 갔는데

덥다
Past: 더웠다 → 더웠는데

When using the future tense ending -(으)ㄹ 것이다, conjugate the verb and attach -ㄴ데 to become -(으)ㄹ 것인데, which can be further shortened to -(으)ㄹ 건데.

가다
Future: 갈 것이다 → 갈 것인데 or 갈 건데

덥다
Future: 더울 것이다 → 더울 것인데 or 더울 건데

From When To When

⊗ **THE WRONG WAY**

1시부터 2시에 거기 있을 거예요.

"I'll be there from one o'clock to two o'clock."

✓ **THE RIGHT WAY**

1시부터 2시까지 거기 있을 거예요.

"I'll be there from one o'clock to two o'clock."

WHY IS THIS WRONG?

Using -에 after 2시 means "at two o'clock," and not "to (until) two o'clock." This sentence would sound like saying, "From one o'clock, at two o'clock I'll be there." This sentence would sound vague and could be confusing.

NEVER MAKE THIS MISTAKE AGAIN

To say "to" and "from" a *time* or *date*, use -부터 ("from") and -까지 ("by," "until"). Note the order that these words go in — "from" comes before "to."

내일까지 오늘부터 일할 거예요. ⊗
오늘부터 내일까지 일할 거예요. ✓
"I'll work from today to tomorrow."

어제 점심부터 새벽 3시까지 드라마를 봤어요.
"I watched dramas from lunchtime yesterday until three in the morning."

지금부터 5시까지 바빠요.
"I'm busy from now until five o'clock."

우리는 6일부터 10일까지 만날 수 있어요.
"We can meet from the sixth to the tenth."

저는 5월부터 7월까지 시간 있어요.
"I have time from May until July."

Note that it's not necessary to use both -부터 and -까지 in every sentence. Feel free to use only one, or both, depending on the meaning you want to convey.

내년까지 한국에서 살 거예요.
"I will live in Korea until next year."

금요일부터 시작했어요.
"I started from Friday."

• • • BONUS EXAMPLES •

| ⊗ | 월요일부터 금요일에 열어요. | | |
| ✓ | 월요일부터 금요일까지 열어요. | Meaning | "We are open from Monday to Friday." |

| ⊗ | 1월부터 3월에 한국에 있을 거예요. | | |
| ✓ | 1월부터 3월까지 한국에 있을 거예요. | Meaning | "I will be in Korea from January until March." |

| ⊗ | 12시부터 1시에 점심시간이에요. | | |
| ✓ | 12시부터 1시까지 점심시간이에요. | Meaning | "Our lunchtime is from twelve to one." |

From Whom To Whom

⊗ **THE WRONG WAY**

제 친구에 선물을 줬어요.

"I gave a present to my friend."

⊘ **THE RIGHT WAY**

제 친구에게 선물을 줬어요.

제 친구한테 선물을 줬어요.

"I gave a present to my friend."

WHY IS THIS WRONG?

-에 means "to," but not when used with a person. This sentence would sound unnatural, since people need to be used with -에게 instead. In addition, the particle 의 also sounds like 에 when spoken, so this sentence could be misunderstood to mean "I gave my friend's present (to someone)."

NEVER MAKE THIS MISTAKE AGAIN

To say "to" and "from" a **person** (or animal), use -에게 ("to") or -에게서 ("from"). The 서 in -에게서 is actually optional, so -에게 can be used for both "to" and "from" — the context of the sentence will make it clear which one you mean.

저에게 주세요.

"Please give it to me."

경화 씨에게 편지를 받았어요.

경화 씨에게서 편지를 받았어요.

"I got a letter from Kyung-hwa."

-한테 ("to") and -한테서 ("from"), which are used in the same way, are more **colloquial** forms.

친구한테 주고 싶어요.

"I want to give it to my friend."

When speaking about someone using *honorific speech*, use -께 ("to," "from")
instead.

선생님께 받았어요.
"I got it from the teacher."

It's also common for Korean learners to misuse -에게/한테 for locations.

학교에게 가고 싶지 않아요. ⊗
학교한테 가고 싶지 않아요. ⊗
학교에 가고 싶지 않아요. ⊘
"I don't want to go to school."

· BONUS EXAMPLES · ·

⊗ 주연 씨에 줄게요.

⊘ 주연 씨에게 줄게요.   Meaning   "I will give it to Jooyeon."

⊘ 주연 씨한테 줄게요.

⊗ 동생에 거짓말했어요.

⊘ 동생에게 거짓말했어요.   Meaning   "I told a lie to my younger
brother/sister."

⊘ 동생한테 거짓말했어요.

⊗ 엄마에 문자 보냈어요.

⊘ 엄마에게 문자 보냈어요.   Meaning   "I sent a text to my mom."

⊘ 엄마한테 문자 보냈어요.

Asking To Someone

⊗ THE WRONG WAY

친구를 전화했어요.

"I called my friend."

⊘ THE RIGHT WAY

친구한테 전화했어요.

"I called my friend."

WHY IS THIS WRONG?

In Korean, you can **call to** someone, but you can't simply **call** someone using the object marker, -을/를. This is because Korean requires you to specify **who** you're calling by adding the word "to."

NEVER MAKE THIS MISTAKE AGAIN

Any Korean verb that shows **communication** (such as calling, telling, or asking) needs to show the person who's receiving that communication with "to." You can use either -에게, -한테, or -께 depending on the level of politeness you want to use. Simply using the object marker, -을/를, would be vague. In Korean, you don't simply "tell someone," "ask someone," or "call someone;" instead, you "tell to someone," "ask to someone," or "call to someone."

저한테 말해 주세요.

"Please tell it to me."

어제 석진 씨한테 전화했어요.

"Yesterday, I called (to) Seok-jin."

누구한테 물어봤어요?

"Who did you ask (to)?"

어제 할머니께 전화 드렸어요.
"I called (to) my grandmother yesterday."

다른 사람한테 비밀번호를 이야기하지 마세요.
"Please don't tell the password to other people."

• • BONUS EXAMPLES •

  ✗ 예지 씨를 물어보세요.

  ✓ 예지 씨한테 물어보세요.

        Meaning   "Ask Yeji."

  ✗ 아빠를 말할 거예요.

  ✓ 아빠한테 말할 거예요.

        Meaning   "I'll tell my dad."

  ✗ 내일 현우 씨를 전화하세요.

  ✓ 내일 현우 씨한테 전화하세요.

        Meaning   "Call Hyunwoo tomorrow."

CHAPTER 75

Seeing And Hearing

⊗ **THE WRONG WAY**

너무 멀어서 아직 볼 수 없어요.

"I can't see it yet because it's too far."

⊘ **THE RIGHT WAY**

너무 멀어서 아직 안 보여요.

"I can't see it yet because it's too far."

WHY IS THIS WRONG?

This sentence is grammatically correct, but it sounds unnatural. While 볼 수 있다 ("to be able to see") makes sense, it's not always the most natural way to say that something can't be seen. There's a shorter and more natural way to say that something isn't **visible**.

NEVER MAKE THIS MISTAKE AGAIN

The **passive verbs** for 보다 ("to see") and 듣다 ("to hear") are 보이다 ("to be seen") and 들리다 ("to be heard"). Passive verbs don't use an object, so when using these verbs, remember to mark the word they're referring to (such as using the Subject Marker or others). An even simpler way to translate these words is "to be visible" and "to be audible." 보이다 and 들리다 can also be used instead of 볼 수 있다 ("to be able to see") and 들을 수 있다 ("to be able to hear"). They're shorter, have the same general meaning, and are more commonly used.

섬을 아직 볼 수 없어요. (less natural)
"I can't see the island still."

섬이 아직 안 보여요. (more natural)
"The island isn't visible yet."
"I can't see the island still."

The difference between using 볼 수 있다 or 들을 수 있다 and 보이다 or 들리다 is this: using 볼 수 있다 and 들을 수 있다 emphasizes that **you** are able (or unable) to do something, while using the passive verbs 보이다 and 들리다 emphasizes that **the subject** itself is what's visible and audible (or not). You might want to use 보이다 and 들리다 instead of 볼 수 있다 and 들을 수 있다 if you don't want someone to think the reason you can't see or hear something is due to your inability to see or hear. In this way, using 보이다 and 들리다 can emphasize that it's not due to your bad vision or hearing.

이제 볼 수 있어요.
"Now I can see (but I couldn't see or wasn't looking before)."

이제 보여요.
"Now I can see (because it's visible)."

네, 소리를 잘 들을 수 있어요.
"Yes, I'm able to hear the sound well."

네, 소리가 잘 들려요.
"Yes, I can hear the sound well (because it's audible)."

저기 저 섬 볼 수 있어요? ⊗
저기 저 섬 보여요? ⊘
"Can you see that island over there?

음악 소리 들을 수 있어요? 저만 들을 수 있는 거 아니죠? ⊗
음악 소리 들리나요? 저만 들리는 거 아니죠? ⊘
"Can you hear the music? It's not only me, right?"

····· BONUS EXAMPLES ·····

Unnatural	Natural	Meaning
글씨가 너무 작아서 볼 수 없어요.	글씨가 너무 작아서 안 보여요.	"The text is so small that I can't see it."

CHAPTER 76

Body Parts Don't Have Emotions

⊗ **THE WRONG WAY**

배가 화났어요.

"My stomach is upset."

⊘ **THE RIGHT WAY**

속이 안 좋아요.

"My stomach is upset."

WHY IS THIS WRONG?

Body parts (such as your stomach) don't have their own emotions. They can cause pain, be uncomfortable, or make sounds, but they don't have existential crises or get jealous. This sentence would sound like your stomach is actually upset at someone.

NEVER MAKE THIS MISTAKE AGAIN

화가 나다 or 화나다 means "upset" or "angry," but is used to describe **emotions**. Body parts (as well as inanimate objects) in Korean don't have emotions, so if you want to say that your stomach is "upset," you'll need to use a different word. You can express this instead by saying that your stomach "hurts," does not feel well, that you're not digesting things well, among other phrases.

배가 화났어요. ⊗
배가 아파요. ⊘
"My stomach hurts (is upset)."

Also, Koreans tend to specify different symptoms by using different expressions. For example, if you feel nauseous, you can say 속이 안 좋다 ("one's insides are not well"). Or if you have an upset stomach that causes you to continually run to the bathroom, you can say 배탈이 나다 ("to have an upset stomach"). Lastly, if you have indigestion you can say 소화가 안 되다 ("digestion doesn't work").

속이 안 좋아요.
"My stomach (inside) isn't well."

배탈(이) 났어요.
"I have an upset stomach."

소화가 안돼요.
"The food isn't sitting well (digesting)."

⊗	경화 씨 배가 화났대요.
⊘	경화 씨가 속이 안 좋대요.

Meaning	"I heard that Kyung-hwa has an upset stomach."

⊗	배가 화나서 점심 안 먹을래요.
⊘	속이 안 좋아서 점심 안 먹을래요.

Meaning	"My stomach is upset, so I'll skip lunch."

⊗	어제부터 배가 화났어요.
⊘	어제부터 속이 안 좋아요.

Meaning	"My stomach has been upset since yesterday."

Don't Translate Literally

⊗ **THE WRONG WAY**

네, 다시 말할 수 있어요.

"Yeah, you can say that again."

⊘ **THE RIGHT WAY**

네, 그 말이 맞아요.

"Yeah, you can say that again."

WHY IS THIS WRONG?

When you want to say something in Korean, such as an expression or idiom, focus on translating the **overall** meaning of the phrase and not its **literal** meaning. There will rarely be an expression or idiom that can be literally translated in Korean and still make sense. Saying this sentence would literally be telling the other person that they're capable of repeating what they said, not that you agree with what they've said.

NEVER MAKE THIS MISTAKE AGAIN

Never **literally** translate from English (or any language) to Korean. Instead, focus on the heart of what you want to say — the underlying overall meaning. Translating the overall meaning will more often give you an accurate translation of any expression that you want to say. In addition, translating an overall meaning will be much simpler than trying to translate the literal meaning of something. Use literal translations when searching for words in the dictionary, and focus on more natural translations when speaking and writing in Korean.

In the example, the heart of the expression "You can say that again." is that you're wholeheartedly agreeing with the other person. To translate it naturally, focus on that aspect of **agreeing** with them. If you do that, you can have several options, such as 맞아요 ("That's right."), 정말 그래요 ("It really is."), among many others.

고양이와 개가 내리고 있어요! ⊗
비가 엄청 많이 오고 있어요! ⊘
"It's raining cats and dogs!"

The heart of the expression "raining cats and dogs" is that it's **pouring** rain — so much that it's astonishing. When trying to translate this phrase, focus on trying to translate that it's raining a lot, not on what specific animals are falling from the sky.

빈대 조심하세요! ⊗
잘 자요! ⊘
"Good night! Don't let the bedbugs bite!"

The heart of the expression "Don't let the bedbugs bite!" is that you're wishing the other person a good night's sleep. Therefore, you should create a natural translation by simply telling them to **sleep well**.

시간이 날아요. ⊗
시간이 금방 가요. ⊘
"Time flies."

The heart of the expression "Time flies." is that time goes by in an instant when you're having fun. Focus on time going quickly, not on it literally **flying**. There could be many ways in Korean to say that time goes by quickly, and any of them should at least make sense.

··· **BONUS EXAMPLES** ···

⊗ 케이크 한 조각이죠.

⊘ 식은 죽 먹기죠.

Meaning   "A piece of cake."

⊗ 제 다리를 당기지 마세요.

⊘ 에이, 설마. 농담하지 마세요.

Meaning   "Don't pull my leg."

Did You Forget?

⊗ THE WRONG WAY

헉! 우산을 잊어버렸어요.

"Oh no! I forgot my umbrella."

⊘ THE RIGHT WAY

헉! 우산을 안 가져왔어요.

"Oh no! I forgot my umbrella."

WHY IS THIS WRONG?

잊다 ("to forget") is used to mean that you've forgotten **something** — specifically, that you've forgotten **about** something. This sentence would sound like you've forgotten the word umbrella, or the existence of an umbrella, but not that you've forgotten to **bring** an umbrella with you.

NEVER MAKE THIS MISTAKE AGAIN

잊다 and 잊어버리다 ("to forget") can be used to say that you forgot about something, but not to say that you forgot **to bring** or **to take** something with you.

놓고 오다 and 놓고 가다 If you want to specify that you've forgotten (left) something **at somewhere**, use 놓고 오다 ("to put down and come") or 놓고 가다 ("to put down and go"). This comes from the verb 놓다 which means "to put down," and literally means that you put something down in a location and then went (가다, 오다, etc.) somewhere else, thereby forgetting it.

집에 카드를 놓고 왔어요.

"I left my card at home (and came here)."

학교에 가방을 놓고 왔어요.

"I left my bag at school (and came here)."

안 가져오다 and 안 가져가다 If you want to specify that you simply didn't **bring** or
take something with you, use 안 가져오다 ("to not take and come") and 안 가져가다
("to not take and go"). This comes from the verb 가지다, which means "to have" or
"to hold on your person," and literally means that you didn't take something with you
before you went somewhere else, thereby forgetting it.

숙제를 안 가져왔어요.
"I forgot (to bring) my homework."

사장님, 돈을 안 가져왔습니다.
"Boss, I forgot (to bring) the money."

···· **BONUS EXAMPLES** ································

⊗   차 키를 잊어버렸어요.

⊘   차 키를 안 가져왔어요.

Meaning   "I forgot my car keys."

⊗   카메라를 잊어버린 것 같아요.

⊘   카메라를 안 가져온 것 같아요.

Meaning   "I guess I forgot my camera."

⊗   테이블에 지갑을 잊어버렸어요!

⊘   테이블에 지갑을 놓고 갔어요!

Meaning   "You forgot your wallet on the table!"

Try To Remember

⊗ **THE WRONG WAY**

이거 기억나 주세요.

"Please remember this."

⊘ **THE RIGHT WAY**

이거 기억해 주세요.

"Please remember this."

WHY IS THIS WRONG?

기억이 나다 or **기억나다** literally means "a memory comes to mind," and can't be used in a command. This sentence would sound like you're asking that a memory return to a person's head, instead of asking that the person tries to remember that memory.

NEVER MAKE THIS MISTAKE AGAIN

기억하다 and 기억나다 both mean "to remember," but have slightly different uses and meanings.

기억하다 This literally means "to remember." It can be used with an object marker, -을/를, to specify what it is that you can't remember. It can be used to say that you remember anything **in general**. However, it can sound a bit stiff (like it came from a textbook).

그 사람을 기억해요.

"I remember that person."

기억나다 This literally means "a memory comes (to mind)." It can be used to mean that a memory comes to your mind, so you remember it. It's not used with an object marker, as 나다 is a **passive verb**; instead, you can use the subject marker, -이/가. If you've suddenly just remembered something (or suddenly don't), use this verb to sound a bit more natural.

그 사람이 기억나요.
"I remember that person."

더이상 기억이 안 나요.
"I don't remember anymore."

이제 기억해. (less natural)
이제 기억나. (more natural)
"I remember now."

However, 기억나다 can't be conjugated with -(으)ㄹ 수 없다 to say that you "can't" remember something. It can only be used to say that you simply "don't" remember.

주소를 기억날 수 없어요. ⊗
주소가 기억이 안 나요. ✓
주소가 기억나지 않아요. ✓
"I can't remember the address."

Also, 기억나다 can't be used when you're **telling** someone to remember something. In this case, use 기억하다 instead.

비밀번호 기억나세요. ⊗
비밀번호 기억하세요. ✓
"Please remember the password."

Besides those two cases, you can use either 기억하다 or 기억나다 in any situation.

BONUS EXAMPLES

⊗ 그 사람 얼굴이 기억날 수 없어요.

✓ 그 사람 얼굴이 기억이 안 나요.

✓ 그 사람 얼굴이 기억나지 않아요.

Meaning   "I can't remember his/her face."

Familiar Names

⊗ **THE WRONG WAY**

아내는 뭐 하세요?

"What does your wife do?"

✓ **THE RIGHT WAY**

아내분은 뭐 하세요?

"What does your wife do?"

WHY IS THIS WRONG?

Korean uses different terms when referring to people who aren't directly related or close to you. To be polite, you shouldn't use 아내 ("wife") when referring to someone else's wife. There are different words for referring to your own wife/husband and someone else's wife/husband.

NEVER MAKE THIS MISTAKE AGAIN

There are different words for referring to your family members depending on whether or not you'd use *honorific speech* toward that person.

아버지 → 아버님 These mean "father." When referring to your own father, you can use either 아빠 ("dad") or 아버지 ("father"), depending on how polite you want to be. When referring to someone else's father who you don't know, or when you want to sound extra polite toward someone else's father, use 아버님. You should also use this whenever you would use *honorific speech* to talk about that father — this same condition applies to all other words in this lesson. You can also use 할아버지 and 할아버님 ("grandfather") in the same way.

어머니 → 어머님 These mean "mother." When referring to your own mother, you can use either 엄마 ("mom") or 어머니 ("mother"). Use 어머님 to refer to someone else's mother whom you want to speak extra politely about. You can also use 할머니 and 할머님 ("grandmother") in the same way.

아들 → 아드님 These mean "son." You can refer to your own son or the son of someone whom you're close with using 아들. When you want to speak extra politely about someone's son, use 아드님.

딸 → 따님 These mean "daughter," and you can use 딸 when referring to your own daughter or the daughter of someone whom you're close with. Use 따님 when referring to a daughter whom you want to speak extra politely about.

아내 → 아내분 These mean "wife," and you can use 아내 when referring to your own wife or the wife of someone whom you're close with. Use 아내분 to show extra respect toward any other wife.

남편 → 남편분 These mean "husband," and you can use 남편 with your own husband or the husband of someone whom you're close with. Use 남편분 to show extra respect toward any other husband.

부모 → 부모님 Although 부모 means "parents," you'll refer to your own parents as 부모님. The word 부모 is only used to refer to "parents" *in general*, and not to any specific set of parents.

There are other terms for different family members, but these are some of the most common ones.

· · BONUS EXAMPLES ·

Inappropriate/Impolite	Appropriate/Polite	Meaning
남편은 어디 계세요?	남편분은 어디 계세요?	"Where is your husband?"
딸이 자랑스러우실 것 같아요.	따님이 자랑스러우실 것 같아요.	"You must be proud of your daughter."

WHY IS THIS SENTENCE AWKWARD OR UNNATURAL?

한국인 친구가 있고 싶어요.

⊘ See Chapter 94

CHAPTER 81

Dear John

⊗ **THE WRONG WAY**

소중한 경은 씨,
감사합니다.
빌리에게서

"Dear Kyeong-eun, Thank you.
From Billy."

⊘ **THE RIGHT WAY**

경은 씨에게,
감사합니다.
빌리 드림

"Dear Kyeong-eun, Thank you.
From Billy."

WHY IS THIS WRONG?

In English, we can address a letter with "Dear," and end it with "From," but Korean doesn't use either of those words when writing letters. This letter would sound like someone used a translation machine or dictionary to translate it one word at a time.

NEVER MAKE THIS MISTAKE AGAIN

There are no rules set in stone for how to write a letter/e-mail in Korean, but here are a few suggestions for how to start and end yours. In Korean, you can start your written letter with the person's **name** or their **title**, then attach -에게 - or -께 when speaking **honorifically**.

철수에게
"Dear Chul-soo···"

아버지께
"Dear Father···"

Use the same sort of politeness that you would use if you were to talk with them, or even a bit more polite depending on the purpose of the letter — avoid any casual speech (and the plain form) with anyone other than close friends.

When writing **honorific speech**, end your letter or e-mail with your name followed by 올림 ("presenting") or 드림 ("giving"). For close friends (casual speech), simply use your name only or your name followed by -(이)가; attach -이가 after a **consonant**, or attach -가 after a **vowel**. This -가 is the subject marker, and is a shortened way of saying "**I** am sending this···." Alternatively, you could also end your letter or e-mail with your name, followed by 씀 ("writing"), when writing casual speech.

김철수 올림
"From Kim Chul-soo"

제시카 드림
"From Jessica"

석진이가
"From Seok-jin"

경화 씀
"From Kyung-hwa"

경은
"From Kyeong-eun"

CHAPTER 82

I Cut My Finger

⊗ **THE WRONG WAY**

요리하다가 손가락을 잘랐어요.

"I cut my finger while cooking."

⊘ **THE RIGHT WAY**

요리하다가 손가락을 베였어요.

"I cut my finger while cooking."

WHY IS THIS WRONG?

Although **자르다** means "to cut," it's only used when you're completely **severing** something. If you were to tell your friend this sentence, they'd wonder why you didn't immediately go to the emergency room.

NEVER MAKE THIS MISTAKE AGAIN

Be careful when using a dictionary to find words — make sure you fully understand their meanings. For example, both 자르다 and 베다 will appear in a dictionary as "to cut," while they have different uses.

자르다 This means "to cut," when you're completely **removing** something. As such, it can also be used when **firing** a person (figuratively cutting them off of the company). In addition, it tends to be used most often when cutting things with scissors more often than with a knife. For example, you could use this verb when getting your hair cut or when cutting a rope.

지금 머리를 자르러 갈 거예요.

"I'm going to get a haircut now."

끈이 너무 두꺼워서 자를 수 없었어요.

"I couldn't cut the rope because it was too thick."

베다 This also means "to cut," and can be used both when **removing** something (cutting a tree, etc.) or when simply **causing injury** to something by cutting it. For example, you should use 베다 if you accidentally cut your hand while cooking, since you've injured your hand and not cut it off. In addition, the verb 베다 is an active verb since it means "to cut," so it could sound like you purposefully cut your finger. Instead, Koreans more often use the passive form of 베다, which is 베이다 ("to be cut").

집에 있는 나무를 전부 베었어요.
"I completely cut down the tree at our house."

면도날에 턱이 베였어요.
"I've got a cut on my chin from the blade."

썰다 This also means "to cut," but it is used most often when cutting things with a knife, especially while cooking.

양파를 잘게 썰어 주세요.
"Please cut the onions into small pieces."

썰어 드릴까요?
"Shall I slice it for you?"

· · · **BONUS EXAMPLES** ·

ⓧ 방금 종이가 손을 잘랐어요.

✓ 방금 종이에 손을 베였어요.

> Meaning "I just got a paper cut."

ⓧ 가위로 베어 주세요.

✓ 가위로 잘라 주세요.

> Meaning "Please cut it with scissors."

How To Clean Everything

⊗ **THE WRONG WAY**

옷을 청소하고 싶어요.

"I want to clean my clothes."

⊘ **THE RIGHT WAY**

옷을 빨고 싶어요.

"I want to clean my clothes."

WHY IS THIS WRONG?

청소하다 means "to clean" something by sweeping and wiping and vacuuming — such as your home. This sentence could sound like you want to perhaps organize your clothes, or wipe them, and would sound unnatural.

NEVER MAKE THIS MISTAKE AGAIN

There are several ways to "clean," depending on what it is you're cleaning.

청소하다 This means "to clean," specifically by wiping, sweeping, or vacuuming. It's used whenever you're cleaning a floor, a room, or an entire home.

오늘 집 청소할 거예요.

"I'll do housecleaning today."

닦다 This means "to wipe," and is used whenever you're cleaning something by wiping or polishing it — such as a table, a toy, or a surface.

차에 묻은 새똥을 다 닦았어요.

"I wiped off all of the bird poop on the car."

빨다 This means "to wash" *clothing*. Specifically, it's used when washing something by rubbing it in water, either by hand or washing machine.

수건을 빨았어요.
"I washed the towel."

씻다 This means "to wash," and is used when washing dirt or oil off the skin using water.

집에 와서 손을 씻었어요.
"I came home and washed my hands."

감다 This means "to wash," and is used when washing your hair.

머리를 계속 감았어요.
"I kept washing my hair."

헹구다 This means "to rinse," and is used whenever you're cleaning something using water, especially in order to remove soap from it.

이불을 물에 잘 헹구세요.
"Rinse the blanket well in water."

세수(를) 하다 This means "to wash," and is used whenever you're washing your *hands* and *face*. As such, this verb can be used to simply mean "to wash up."

오늘은 세수만 하고 나왔어요.
"I only washed my hands and face before I came here."

• • • BONUS EXAMPLES •

⊗ 아침에 머리 씻었어요?

✓ 아침에 머리 감았어요?

Meaning "Did you wash your hair this morning?."

Irregular ㅂ Verbs

⊗ **THE WRONG WAY**

이 음식은 너무 맵어요.

"This food is too spicy."

⊘ **THE RIGHT WAY**

이 음식은 너무 매워요.

"This food is too spicy."

WHY IS THIS WRONG?

Each verb has its own conjugation rules, depending on the type of the verb and the verb stem. 맵다 ("to be spicy") has specific rules due to the ㅂ at the bottom of the verb stem, and conjugating it wrong will sound unnatural.

NEVER MAKE THIS MISTAKE AGAIN

Korean verbs conjugate differently depending on their type — action verb or descriptive verb — and their verb stems. Most verbs, although they may be called **irregular**, actually are very regular and conjugate according to rules. Some verbs (such as ones with ㅂ) are often irregular.

Consonant ㅂ

One commonly misused verb type is ㅂ verbs — verb stems that end with a single ㅂ. Before starting to conjugate a verb, first look at the verb stem, which is the remaining part of a verb after removing the 다 from the very end. For 하다, this is 하, and for 가르치다, this is 가르치. If the verb stem ends with ㅂ, keep reading.

For the majority of **descriptive verbs**, remove the ㅂ and attach 우. Next, attach ㅓ (which will combine with 우 to become 워). Finally, attach 요.

맵다 → 맵 → 매 → 매우 → 매워(요)

아름답다 → 아름답 → 아름다 → 아름다우 → 아름다워(요)
부럽다 → 부럽 → 부러 → 부러우 → 부러워(요)
귀엽다 → 귀엽 → 귀여 → 귀여우 → 귀여워(요)
춥다 → 춥 → 추 → 추우 → 추워(요)
새롭다 → 새롭 → 새로 → 새로우 → 새로워(요)
덥다 → 덥 → 더우 → 더워(요)

Many *action verb stems* ending with ㅂ will be irregular. Most conjugate like normal verbs, by attaching 아 (for verb stems ending with ㅏ or ㅗ) or 어 (for all other verb stems). Others will conjugate just like descriptive verbs (with 워). And others will conjugate by removing the ㅂ and attaching 와 (instead of 워).

뽑다 → 뽑 (ㅗ) → 뽑아(요)
입다 → 입 (ㅣ) → 입어(요)
눕다 → 눕 → 누 → 누우 → 누워(요)
줍다 → 줍 → 주 → 주우 → 주워(요)
돕다 → 돕 → 도 → 도오 → 도와(요)

Other Irregulars There are other verbs using ㅂ that will be irregular, such as the descriptive verbs 곱다 ("to be kind-hearted"), which becomes 고와(요), and 좁다 ("to be narrow"), which becomes 좁아(요), among others.

⋯ BONUS EXAMPLES ⋯

(×) 너무 귀엽어요.

(✓) 너무 귀여워요.

> Meaning "It's so cute."

(×) 너무 춥어서 롱패딩 입었어요.

(✓) 너무 추워서 롱패딩 입었어요.

> Meaning "It was so cold that I put on a long padded jacket."

CHAPTER 85

Looking Forward To It

(×) **THE WRONG WAY**

정말 흥분해요!

"I'm really excited!"

(✓) **THE RIGHT WAY**

정말 기대돼요!

"I'm really excited!"

WHY IS THIS WRONG?

흥분하다 means "to be excited," but it shouldn't be used when you're simply *looking forward to* something. It means that you're *excited* and *worked up* — perhaps even aroused.

NEVER MAKE THIS MISTAKE AGAIN

흥분하다 Koreans use 흥분하다 when someone is *extremely* excited about something, perhaps to the point of *overreacting* — such as if they're excited *romantically* (aroused) or *emotionally*. Therefore, it is often used in negative sentences.

흥분하지 마세요.

"Don't lose your temper (don't get too excited)."

흥분되다 This can be used when someone is extremely excited about something, but in a positive way. Alternatively, you could use the expression 설레다 to give off a milder, more romantic meaning of feeling excited.

여행 갈 생각하니까 흥분돼서 잠이 안 와요.

"I am so excited thinking about the trip that I can't fall asleep."

이따가 그 사람 만날 건데 벌써부터 설레요.

"I am going to meet him/her later, but my heart is already fluttering (I already feel so excited)."

기대되다 This means "to look forward to" or "to expect." It's typically only used in the **present tense**. This form will not use the object marker, -을/를, when specifying what you're looking forward to.

콘서트가 정말 기대돼요!
"I'm really looking forward to the concert!"

Also, note that you can use this form to say that you "can't wait" for something (because you're looking forward to it).

기다릴 수 없어요! ⊗
기대돼요! ⊘
"I can't wait!"

기대하다: This also means "to look forward to" or "to expect." It can be used in any tense, except for the simple present tense, 기대해요 (which sounds awkward). This form can use the object marker to specify what you're looking forward to.

내일 모임을 기대해요. ⊗
내일 모임을 기대하고 있어요. ⊘
"I'm looking forward to tomorrow's meeting."
내일 모임을 기대할게요. ⊘
"I will look forward to tomorrow's meeting."

기대했던 만큼 재미있지는 않았어요.
"It wasn't as fun as I expected."

Break A Leg!

⊗ **THE WRONG WAY**

어제 다리를 깼어요.

"I broke my leg yesterday."

⊘ **THE RIGHT WAY**

어제 다리가 부러졌어요.

"I broke my leg yesterday."

WHY IS THIS WRONG?

깨다 ("to break") is used for breaking or smashing objects, but isn't used when you've accidentally broken a bone. If you say that you broke your leg using 깨다, it might sound like you took your leg bone in your hands and smashed it into pieces on the ground.

NEVER MAKE THIS MISTAKE AGAIN

Although it would make sense to say that you broke a bone using 깨지다, it would sound like your bone shattered into a bunch of pieces — not that it simply fractured. Here are some of the ways to say "break" in Korean:

깨다 This means "to break" or "to smash into pieces." It can be used with an object marker -을/를 to specify what you broke.

유리를 깼어요.

"I broke the glass."

깨지다 This means "to be broken" or "to be smashed into pieces," and can't be used with an object marker. It is short for 깨어지다.

유리가 깨졌어요.

"The glass broke."

부러뜨리다 This means "to fracture" (such as a bone), and can be used with an object marker to specify what you fractured.

연필 부러뜨리지 마세요.
"Please don't break the pencil."

부러지다 This means "to be fractured," and can't be used with an object marker.

운동하다가 팔이 부러졌어요.
"I broke my arm while exercising."

⊗ 컵을 부러뜨렸어요.

✓ 컵을 깼어요.

Meaning "I broke the cup."

⊗ 팔이 깨진 것 같아요.

✓ 팔이 부러진 것 같아요.

Meaning "I think my arm is broken."

⊗ 칫솔이 깨졌어요.

✓ 칫솔이 부러졌어요.

Meaning "My toothbrush is broken."

CHAPTER 87

Answering Negative Questions

⊗ **THE WRONG WAY**

A: **TV 보는 거 안 좋아하죠?**

"You don't like watching TV, right?"

B: **아니요. 안 좋아해요.**

"No, I don't like it."

⊘ **THE RIGHT WAY**

A: **TV 안 좋아하죠?**

"You don't like watching TV, right?"

B: **네. 안 좋아해요.**

"Yes, I don't like it."

WHY IS THIS WRONG?

In English, we can answer "yes" or "no" depending on the type of response we're going to give — "No, I dislike it" or "Yes, I like it." In Korean, negative questions are answered more literally than they are in English. Answering "no" to a negative question would mean you're disagreeing with the other person.

NEVER MAKE THIS MISTAKE AGAIN

When someone asks you a negative question (one that uses 안 or -지 않다), respond according to whether that negative verb is correct or not. For example, if someone asks if you *dislike* something (싫어하다), answer according to the verb 싫어하다 and not according to your answer. If you do dislike it, answer "Yes," or if someone asks if you *don't want* to go somewhere (가고 싶지 않다), then answering "Yes" means you're agreeing you don't want to go. If you answer "No," it means "No, I *do want* to go."

A: 배 안 고파요?
"Aren't you hungry?"

B: 아니요. 배 안 고파요. ⊗
B: 네. 배 안 고파요. ⊘
"Yes, I'm not hungry."

A: 영어 못해요?

"You are not good at English?"

B: 아니요. 못해요. ⊗

B: 네. 못해요. ⊘

"Yes, I am not."

A: 지금은 안 될까요?

"Is now not okay?"

B: 네. 지금 돼요. ⊗

B: 네. 지금은 안 될 것 같아요. ⊘

"Yes, I don't think I can do it now."

• • • **BONUS EXAMPLES** •

⊗ A: 우산 없어요?
　 B: 아니요. 없어요.

⊘ A: 우산 없어요?
　 B: 네. 없어요.

Meaning　A: "You don't have an umbrella?"
　　　　　B: "Yes, I don't."

⊗ A: 예지 씨는 안 가요?
　 B: 아니요. 안 가요.

⊘ A: 예지 씨는 안 가요?
　 B: 네. 안 가요.

Meaning　A: "Yeji, you are not coming (with us)?"
　　　　　B: "Yes, I'm not."

⊗ A: 여기 들어가면 안 돼요?
　 B: 네. 돼요.

⊘ A: 여기 들어가면 안 돼요?
　 B: 아니요. 돼요.

Meaning　A: "We are not allowed to go in here?"
　　　　　B: "No, you are."

Too Many

많이 사람들이 집에 왔어요.

"Many people came to the house."

많은 사람들이 집에 왔어요.
사람들이 집에 많이 왔어요.

"Many people came to the house."

WHY IS THIS WRONG?

많이 is an *adverb*, and can only be used before a *verb* — it can't be used as an adjective directly before a noun. This sentence would sound unnatural, like saying "People a lot came to the house."

NEVER MAKE THIS MISTAKE AGAIN

There are several forms of the verb 많다 ("to be many," "to be a lot"), depending on how it's being used:

많이 This can be used as an *adverb* (directly before a verb).

많은 좋아해요. ⊗
많이 좋아해요. ⊘

"I like it a lot."

돈이 많은 없어요. ⊗
돈이 많이 없어요. ⊘

"There isn't much money."

많은 This can be used as an *adjective* (directly before a noun).

많이 선생님들도 안 좋아해요. ⊗
많은 선생님들도 안 좋아해요. ⊘

"A lot of teachers don't like it either."

문제가 많이 친구가 있어요. ⊗
문제가 많은 친구가 있어요. ⊘
"I have a friend with a lot of problems."

많다 This can be conjugated as a regular *descriptive verb*.

질문이 너무 많은. ⊗
질문이 너무 많아요. ⊘
"There are too many questions."

⊗ 많이 설탕 들어 있어요.

⊘ 많은 설탕이 들어 있어요. (written)　　Meaning　"There's a lot of sugar in it."

⊘ 설탕이 많이 들어 있어요. (spoken)

⊗ 많은 그런 질문 받아요.　　Meaning　"I get asked that question a lot."

⊘ 그런 질문 많이 받아요.

CHAPTER 89

Are You A Shy Person?

⊗ **THE WRONG WAY**

아기가 많이 부끄러워해요.

"The baby is very shy."

⊘ **THE RIGHT WAY**

아기가 부끄러움이 많아요.

아기가 부끄러움을 많이 타요.

"The baby is very shy."

WHY IS THIS WRONG?

부끄럽다 means "to be shy" or "to be embarrassed," but needs to be changed into an action verb — **부끄러워하다** — whenever the subject (whoever feels shy or embarrassed) is a third person; this is the same concept we learned in Chapter 63. However, this verb is only used when describing a moment or time when someone was shy or embarrassed. Instead, if you want to say that someone is a shy person *in general*, you need to say it differently.

NEVER MAKE THIS MISTAKE AGAIN

If you want to say that someone is a shy person in general, there are several expressions that you can use:

부끄러움이 많다 부끄러움 is the noun form of 부끄럽다, and literally means "shyness." Koreans can say that someone "has a lot of shyness" when they are a shy person.

저는 부끄러움이 많은 편이에요.

"I tend to be very shy."

부끄러움을 많이 타다 타다 here means "to feel," so 부끄러움을 많이 타다 literally means "to feel a lot of shyness" or "to feel shyness easily." This expression is also commonly used by Koreans.

저는 부끄러움을 많이 타는 편이에요.
"I tend to be very shy."

You can also replace 부끄러움 with another synonym of it, such as 쑥스러움 or 수줍음.

저는 부끄러움이 많은 편이에요.
저는 쑥스러움이 많은 편이에요.
저는 수줍음이 많은 편이에요.
"I tend to be very shy."

낯(을) 가리다 낯 means "face," and 가리다 means "to distinguish" or "to be picky," so this literally translates as "to distinguish faces" or "to be picky about faces." This is most often used when someone, especially a baby, is shy around strangers. The noun form of 낯(을) 가리다 is 낯가림, and people will also often say 낯가림이 심하다 (literally, "one's shyness is severe.").

경화는 낯을 별로 안 가려요.
"Kyung-hwa is not really shy (around people)."

저희 애는 낯가림이 심해요.
"My baby is very shy around strangers."

· · **BONUS EXAMPLES** ·

Unnatural	Natural	Meaning
저는 많이 부끄러워하는 성격이에요.	저는 부끄러움을 많이 타는 성격이에요.	"I'm a very shy person."
많이 부끄러워하는 아이예요?	부끄러움이 많은 아이예요?	"Is this kid a shy person?"

CHAPTER 90

Saying Yes

ⓧ **THE WRONG WAY**

네. 좋아.

"Yes, that's good."

✓ **THE RIGHT WAY**

네. 좋아요. / 응. 좋아.

"Yes, that's good."

WHY IS THIS WRONG?

There's more than one way to say "yes," and using 네 is *polite*. When using 네 with *casual speech*, it will either sound impolite to someone who's older or awkward to a friend.

NEVER MAKE THIS MISTAKE AGAIN

There are several ways to say "yes" in Korean:

네 This is the most *polite* way to say "yes". Some people also say 예. Note that replying with only "yes" and nothing else can sound impolite in some cases (such as formal situations), so use it at the start of a sentence that fully answers the question.

A: 다 했어요?
"Did you finish it?"

B: 네. *(less polite/formal)*
"Yes."

B: 네. 다 했어요. *(more polite/formal)*
"Yes. I finished it."

응 This is the *casual* way to say "yes", and should only be used when speaking casually — such as with friends and close acquaintances. Alternatively, you can also say 어 with close friends.

A: 밥 먹었어?
"Did you eat?"

B: 네. 이미 먹었어. ⊗
"Yes, I already ate."

B: 응. 이미 먹었어. ⊘
"Yes, I already ate."

• • BONUS EXAMPLES •

When A and B are close friends:

⊗ A: 집에 잘 도착했어?
　 B: 네. 잘 도착했어.

⊘ A: 집에 잘 도착했어?
　 B: 응. 잘 도착했어.

Meaning
A: "Did you arrive home safely?"
B: "Yes, I arrived home safely."

⊗ A: 이거 맛있어?
　 B: 네. 맛있어.

⊘ A: 이거 맛있어?
　 B: 응. 맛있어.

Meaning
A: "Does this taste good?"
B: "Yes, it does."

⊗ A: 많이 피곤해?
　 B: 네. 너무 피곤해.

⊘ A: 많이 피곤해?
　 B: 응. 너무 피곤해.

Meaning
A: "Are you very tired?"
B: "Yes, I'm so tired."

Saying No

ⓧ **THE WRONG WAY**

저는 한국 사람 아니요.

"I'm not a Korean."

⊘ **THE RIGHT WAY**

저는 한국 사람이 아니에요.

"I'm not a Korean."

WHY IS THIS WRONG?

아니요 means "no," and is a single *word* you can use when replying to a question. It doesn't mean "not," so this sentence would sound like, "I Korean person no."

NEVER MAKE THIS MISTAKE AGAIN

There are several ways to say "no" in Korean.

아니요 This is a *polite* way to say "no". Note that only replying with "no" and nothing else can sound impolite in some cases (such as formal situations), so remember to answer "no" at the start of a sentence that fully explains your answer. In *casual speech*, you can use 아니.

A: 이거 좋아해요?
"Do you like this?"

B: 아니요. *(less polite/formal)*
"No."

B: 아니요. 안 좋아해요. *(more polite/formal)*
"No, I don't like it."

A: 지금 바빠?
"Are you busy now?"

B: 아니. 안 바빠.
"No, I'm not."

아니다 This is a ***descriptive verb*** that means "to not be," and is used after a noun to say that something is ***not*** a certain way. It is not used to say "no," but can be used to specify what someone or something ***is not***. It can be conjugated several ways, including 아니야 (for ***casual speech***), 아니에요 (for ***polite speech***), and 아닙니다 (for ***formal speech***).

A: 혹시 현우 씨예요?
"Are you Hyunwoo by any chance?"

B: 아니요. 아니에요.
"No, I'm not (Hyunwoo)."

Be careful not to confuse 아니요 with 아니에요. 아니요 (or 아니) is used to say "no" to what someone has said, while 아니에요 (or any of its other forms) is used to say that something or someone ***is not*** a certain way.

파리 아니요! 말벌이에요! ⊗
파리 아니에요! 말벌이에요! ⊘
"It's not a fly! It's a wasp!"

••• **BONUS EXAMPLES** ••••••••••••••••••••••••••

⊗
A: 이거 먹어도 돼요?
B: 이거 먹는 거 아니요.

⊘
A: 이거 먹어도 돼요?
B: 이거 먹는 거 아니에요.

Meaning

A: "Can I eat this?"
B: "It's not something to eat."

CHAPTER 92

Spelling Matters Too

ⓧ **THE WRONG WAY**

저도 학생이예요.

"I'm a student too."

✓ **THE RIGHT WAY**

저도 학생이에요.

"I'm a student too."

WHY IS THIS WRONG?

-이다 can be conjugated to the 요 form as either -이에요 or -예요, but it's commonly misspelled in various other ways. Using the wrong spelling of words (such as -이예요) can cause your Korean writing to look strange and unprofessional.

NEVER MAKE THIS MISTAKE AGAIN

Many words in Korean are commonly misspelled — both by learners of Korean and native Korean speakers. While most situations won't require perfect spelling (such as writing messages to friends), some situations do, such as writing essays and reports or for doing any work in Korean.

-이다 In the 요 form, this conjugates as -이에요 after a *consonant* or as -예요 after a *vowel*. However, -예요 is most often pronounced as -에요, which is what leads to this word being commonly misspelled.

여기가 저희 학교에요. ⓧ
여기가 저희 학교예요. ✓
"Here is my school."

같다 In the 요 form, this conjugates as 같아요. It's also commonly pronounced as 같애요, which is a common colloquial pronunciation.

그런 것 같애요. ⊗
그런 것 같아요. ✓
"I think so."

바라다 In the 요 form, this conjugates as 바라요. It's more often pronounced as 바래요, but should be written as 바라요.

시험 잘 되길 바래요. ⊗
시험 잘 되길 바라요. ✓
"I hope your test goes well."

-(으)ㄹ게(요) This form is used when saying that you'll do something for someone else, or when you're responding to something someone asked you. For this form, take a verb stem and attach -을게(요) after a **consonant**, or attach -ㄹ게(요) after a **vowel**. Due to sound change rules between ㄹ and 게, 게요 is **pronounced** as 께요. However, it should only be written as 게요.

지금 갈께요! ⊗
지금 갈게요! ✓
"I'm going now!"

되다: In the 요 form, this conjugates as 돼요.

컴퓨터가 안 되요. ⊗
컴퓨터가 안 돼요. ✓
"The computer doesn't work."

There are many more common mistakes, but these are some of the simpler ones. However, you choose to use these words in casual conversation — just be aware of their correct spellings and pronunciation when necessary.

Through Doing

⊗ **THE WRONG WAY**

친구로써 충고할게.

"Let me advise you as a friend."

⊘ **THE RIGHT WAY**

친구로서 충고할게.

"Let me advise you as a friend."

WHY IS THIS WRONG?

This isn't only a small spelling mistake. Both -**로써** and -**로서** are real grammar forms, but have different uses and meanings. Using **친구로써** actually means something like "through a friend," not "as a friend."

NEVER MAKE THIS MISTAKE AGAIN

The two similar-sounding forms -로서 and -로써 have completely different uses.

-(으)로서 Use this form to do something "as" someone; for example, "as a parent," "as a teacher," or "as a friend." To use this, take a noun and attach -으로서 if it ends in a *consonant*, or attach -로서 if it ends in a *vowel*. Note that the 서 is optional.

부모로서 도와줘야 돼요.

"I have to help as a parent."

친구로서 걱정돼요.

"I'm worried as a friend."

한국어를 공부하는 사람으로서 이해할 수 있어요.

"I can understand it as someone who's studying Korean."

-(으)로써 Use this form to do something "with" or "by means of" something. To use this, take a noun and attach -으로써 if it ends in a *consonant*, or attach -로써 if it ends in a *vowel*.

말로써 표현할 수가 없어요.
"I can't express it with words."

-(으)ㅁ으로써 Use this form to do something "through" or "by way of" doing an
action verb. For example, you can learn Korean "through studying." To use this, take
an action verb stem and attach -음으로써 if it ends in a *consonant*, or attach -ㅁ으로
써 if it ends in a *vowel*.

Note that -(으)ㅁ으로써 is mostly only used in formal Korean or written text.

이렇게 함으로써 경비를 줄일 수 있었습니다.
"By doing this, we were able to reduce expenses."

Remember that this is **only** how to say "through" when using an action verb, not a
noun; for that, use 통해(서) after a noun.

친구 통해서 들었어요.
"I heard it through a friend."

· · · BONUS EXAMPLES ·

ⓧ 선생님으로써 그런 행동은 할 수 없어요.

✓ 선생님으로서 그런 행동은 할 수 없어요.

Meaning   "As a teacher, I cannot do such behavior."

ⓧ 엄마로써 한마디만 할게.

✓ 엄마로서 한마디만 할게.

Meaning   "As your mother, let me say one thing."

Want It To

너무 추워요. 봄이 오고 싶어요.

"It's too cold. I want spring to come."

너무 추워요. 봄이 왔으면 좋겠어요.

"It's too cold. I want spring to come."

WHY IS THIS WRONG?

The -고 싶다 ending can only be used to say that you want **to do** something yourself or that someone else wants to. It can't be used to say that you want someone or something else to do something. This sentence would sound like saying, "Spring wants to come," which is also awkward since seasons don't have wants.

NEVER MAKE THIS MISTAKE AGAIN

To say that you want someone or something else to do something, combine the -(으)면 form ("if" or "when") together with 좋겠다 ("it would be good···"). Together, -(으)면 좋겠다 literally means "If (something or someone does something), it would be good." This is a natural way to say "I wish···," "I hope...," or "I want···" for something to happen. The verb used with -(으)면 can be in the **present tense** or in the **past tense**; both have the same meaning.

빨리 방학하면 좋겠다!
빨리 방학했으면 좋겠다!
"I wish (summer/winter) vacation would come soon!"

수업이 지금 끝났으면 좋겠어요.
"I wish the class would finish now."

친구가 도와주면 좋겠는데.
"I wish my friend would help."

저한테도 이야기했으면 좋겠어요.
"I wish you'd tell me too."

In addition to ***doing something*** using action verb, you can also use this form after descriptive verbs.

내일 날씨가 좋았으면 좋겠어요.
"I hope the weather is nice tomorrow."

영화가 재미있으면 좋겠어요.
"I hope the movie is entertaining."

· · · **BONUS EXAMPLES** ·

⊗ 눈이 오고 싶어요.

⊘ 눈이 왔으면 좋겠어요.

> Meaning — "I want it to snow."

⊗ 한국인 친구가 있고 싶어요.

⊘ 한국인 친구가 있었으면 좋겠어요.

> Meaning — "I want to have a Korean friend."

⊗ 비가 그치고 싶어요.

⊘ 비가 그쳤으면 좋겠어요.

> Meaning — "I want the rain to stop."

You Wanna?

─────────────────────────────

⊗ THE WRONG WAY

경화 씨도 같이 먹고 싶어요?

"Do you want to eat together, Kyung-hwa?"

⊘ THE RIGHT WAY

경화 씨도 같이 먹을래요?

"Do you want to eat together, Kyung-hwa?"

WHY IS THIS WRONG?

Grammatically, it's perfectly fine to ask someone if they want to do something using the **-고 싶다** form. However, this form focuses on the action itself (that Kyung-hwa wants to eat), not that a person *intends* to (or plans to) do something. It would be a bit more natural to ask if Kyung-hwa *is going to* eat together with you than simply if she *wants* to eat.

─────────────────────────────

NEVER MAKE THIS MISTAKE AGAIN

There are two forms for saying "want to" when used with an *action verb*. Although both can be used in most situations, they're slightly different. In some cases, one or the other will be preferred.

-고 싶다 This is the most standard way to say that you "want to" *do something*. It can be used in formal and informal situations. Note that this is not how you can say that you simply "want" something. To use it, take an *action verb stem* and attach -고 싶다, and conjugate it.

한국어 배우고 싶어요.

"I want to learn Korean."

이 음식 먹어 보고 싶어요.

"I want to try (eating) this food."

In addition to the object marker, 을/를, it is also okay to use the subject marker, 이/가, to talk about what you want to do. Doing this puts more emphasis on what it is that you want to do.

저는 삼겹살을 먹고 싶어요.
저는 삼겹살이 먹고 싶어요.
"I want to eat pork belly."

-(으)ㄹ래(요) This is an *informal* way to say that you "want to" do something; it shouldn't be used when you want to sound extra polite. This form also has one more usage — when saying that you *intend* to do something or that you're *going to* do something. For example, you can use this form when asking your friend if they're going to a concert (if they *intend to go*). In this way, it is more than simply asking if someone wants to do an action verb; it's asking them if they also *will* do that or *intend* to do that. To use it, take an *action verb stem* and attach -을래(요) if it ends in a *consonant*, or attach -ㄹ래(요) if it ends in a *vowel*. Verb stems ending in ㄹ will drop the ㄹ first.

한국어 배울래요.
"I want to learn Korean."
"I intend to learn Korean."
"I'm going to learn Korean."

내일 콘서트에 갈래요?
"Do you want to go to the concert tomorrow?"
"Do you intend to go to the concert tomorrow?"
"Are you going to the concert tomorrow?"

· · BONUS EXAMPLES ·

Unnatural	Natural	Meaning
커피 마시러 같이 가고 싶어요?	커피 마시러 같이 갈래요?	"Do you want to come with us for coffee?"

It's Unfortunately Incorrect

불행하게도 그 제품은 품절되었습니다.

"Unfortunately, that product is sold out."

안타깝게도 그 제품은 품절되었습니다.

"Unfortunately, that product is sold out."

WHY IS THIS WRONG?

There are two main ways of saying "unfortunately," and 불행하게도 is not commonly used. Since 불행하게도 sounds too dramatic, it's not the most natural way to express regret for something.

NEVER MAKE THIS MISTAKE AGAIN

There are two ways to say "unfortunately," and both are *adverbs*:

불행하게도 This comes from the descriptive verb 불행하다, which means "to not be happy." This is the antonym of 행복하다 ("to be happy"). Koreans typically use the word 행복 ("happiness") to describe a specific moment when they feel happy — even for simple or trivial moments. However, Koreans don't often use the word 불행 ("unhappiness") when describing trivial sad or unhappy moments, and instead, tend to use it for larger, more tragic events. Therefore, 불행하게도 sounds like something "unfortunately" and "tragically" occurred, and you will likely only find it used in writing.

불행하게도 그는 재산을 모두 잃었다.

"Unfortunately, he lost all his property."

안타깝게도 This comes from the descriptive verb 안타깝다, which means "to be regrettable." A natural way to translate this is also "to be too bad." This is a much more natural way to say "unfortunately," as it shows *regret* about something. It can be used in any situation.

안타깝게도 이 영화는 매진이에요.
"Unfortunately, the tickets for this movie are all sold out."

안타깝게도 이렇게 됐네요.
"Unfortunately, it turned out this way."

안타깝다 can also be used by itself as a descriptive verb.

안타깝네요.
"That's regrettable."
"That's too bad."

Unnatural	Natural	Meaning
불행하게도 저희 팀이 졌어요.	안타깝게도 저희 팀이 졌어요.	"Unfortunately, our team lost."
불행하게도 저는 오늘 회의에 참석 못 할 것 같아요	안타깝게도 저는 오늘 회의에 참석 못 할 것 같아요.	"Unfortunately, I don't think I can attend today's meeting."
불행하게도 그 사람과는 연락이 안 돼요.	안타깝게도 그 사람과는 연락이 안 돼요.	"Unfortunately, I can't reach him/her."

For Me And You

ⓧ **THE WRONG WAY**

저를 위해서 눈을 안 좋아해요.

"For me, I don't like snow."

✓ **THE RIGHT WAY**

저는 눈을 안 좋아해요.

"For me, I don't like snow."

WHY IS THIS WRONG?

This is a common mistake that can happen after learning the **위해(서)** form, and it has to do with literally translating English. This sentence would sound like saying "For the purpose of me, it was not very good."

NEVER MAKE THIS MISTAKE AGAIN

The grammar form 위해(서) means "for," but it has a specific usage. It can't be used to translate the word "for" in every situation. 위해(서) really means "for the purpose of," and is used when you want to say that something or someone is "for" something or someone else.

내년 시험을 위해서 지금부터 공부할 거예요.

"I will study from now on for (the purpose of) the test next year."

이 음식은 저를 위한 거예요.

"This food is for me."

When simply expressing your opinion, don't use 위해(서). Actually, you don't need to use 한테 or anything special. We learned that the topic marker, -은/는, can be used to mean "As for…" or "When it comes to…" when used after a noun. It can also be used just to mean "for" with a person - 저는 or 나는 can also translate to "For me…."

저는 완벽하다고 생각해요.
"For me, I think it's perfect."

저는 스테이크 주세요.
"For me, please give me steak."

Again, don't use 위해(서) for every situation where you'd say "for" It should only be used to mean "for the purpose of." Using it for other cases can easily be wrong.

이 책(을) 위해서 감사합니다. ⊗
이 책(을) 주셔서 감사합니다. ⊘
"Thank you for (giving me) this book."

Alternatively, you can say "to me." To say "to," you can use -한테는 (or less commonly, -에게는).

저한테는 그 영화가 명작이에요.
"To me, that movie is a masterpiece."

저한테는 너무 신기해요.
"To me, it's so cool."

나한테는 이 옷이 좀 커.
"To me, these clothes are a bit big."

· · · BONUS EXAMPLES ·

⊗ 저를 위해서 좋은 생각인 것 같아요.

⊘ 저는 좋은 생각인 것 같아요.

> Meaning

"For me, I think it's a good idea."

⊗ 저를 위해서 중국 음식 먹고 싶어요.

⊘ 저는 중국 음식 먹고 싶어요.

> Meaning

"For me, I would like to have Chinese food."

All The While

⊗ THE WRONG WAY

철수가 청소를 하면서
저는 숙제를 했어요.

"I did my homework while Chul-soo cleaned."

⊘ THE RIGHT WAY

철수가 청소를 하는 동안에
저는 숙제를 했어요.

"I did my homework while Chul-soo cleaned."

WHY IS THIS WRONG?

Although -(으)면서 means "while," it can't be used with two different subjects. Saying this sentence would sound like saying saying an incomplete sentence — "Chul-soo, while doing cleaning···. As for me, I did my homework."

NEVER MAKE THIS MISTAKE AGAIN

There are two ways to say "while," and both are important to know:

Verb Stem + -(으)면서

Use this form to say "while" when the same subject (person) is doing everything in the sentence. This form is conjugated the exact same way as -(으)면, with the addition of 서 at the end. Take a verb stem and attach -으면서 if it ends in a **consonant**, or attach -면서 if it ends in a **vowel**.

저는 석진 씨하고 이야기하면서 숙제를 했어요.
"I did my homework while talking with Seok-jin."

사이다를 마시면서 TV를 봤어요.
"I watched TV while drinking soda."

라디오를 들으면서 한국어를 공부했어요.
"I studied Korean while listening to the radio."

신발을 신으면서 친구에게 문자를 보내고 있어요.
"I'm sending texts to my friend while putting on my shoes."

Action Verb Stem + -는 동안(에)

Use this form to say "while" when a different subject (person) is doing something. The 에 at the end is optional. In addition, this form can also be used when the same subject is doing everything, although -(으)면서 is usually preferred.

제가 쉬고 있는 동안에 동생은 밖에서 놀고 있었어요.
"While I was resting, my younger sibling was playing outside."

제가 삼겹살을 굽는 동안에 누나가 설거지를 했어요.
"While I was grilling pork belly, my sister did the dishes."

라디오를 듣는 동안 한국어를 공부했어요.
"I studied Korean while listening to the radio."

· BONUS EXAMPLES ·

✗ 너 TV 보면서 나는 숙제 다 했어.	
✓ 너 TV 보는 동안에 나는 숙제 다 했어.	Meaning "While you were watching TV, I finished my homework."

✗ 너 나갈 준비하면서 나는 좀 더 잘게.	
✓ 너 나갈 준비하는 동안 나는 좀 더 잘게.	Meaning "While you are getting ready to go out, I'll sleep more."

CHAPTER 99

The Busiest Store

⊗ THE WRONG WAY

이 버스는 바빠요.

"This bus is busy."

⊘ THE RIGHT WAY

이 버스에는 사람이 많아요.

"This bus is busy."

WHY IS THIS WRONG?

바쁘다 ("to be busy") can't be used for inanimate objects like buses. Saying that a bus is busy would sound like it has a life and is trying to find time to go to college while raising a kid. (You can do it, bus.)

NEVER MAKE THIS MISTAKE AGAIN

"Busy" doesn't always mean "busy," and there are several ways to say "busy" depending on what it is that you're talking about:

바쁘다 This means "to be busy," and means that someone has a lot of things they need to do. It's only used when talking about a person (or an animal that has a lot of things to do).

지금은 너무 바빠요. 내일 만날 수 있을까요?

"I'm too busy now. Could we meet tomorrow?"

현우 씨가 바쁜 척을 하고 있어요.

"Hyunwoo is pretending to be busy."

사람이 많다 This literally means "there are a lot of people," and is a common way to say that a *location* is "busy." It can be used whenever there are a lot of people anywhere.

홍대에는 항상 사람이 많아요.
"There is always a lot of people in Hongdae."

여기 사람이 진짜 많아서 지나갈 수도 없어요.
"There are so many people here that I can't even get through."

복잡하다 This means "to be complicated," and is useful for describing locations that are so busy and so crowded that they become *complicated* to get around in. This could be a road/street, a subway, or a transit station.

이 길은 너무 복잡해요.
"This road/street is too crowded."

지하철은 복잡해서 싫어요. 그냥 택시를 타고 갈게요.
"I don't like the subway because it's busy. I'll just take a taxi there."

붐비다 This means "to be crowded," and is used to describe that there are many people or vehicles moving around in a small space. You can think of this as meaning "to be bustling."

여기는 밤에만 붐벼요.
"It's only bustling here in the nighttime."

From time to time, you might hear Koreans describe certain places, such as stores, as 바쁘다. This is because they are picturing the people inside of the store or what they are doing, rather than the store itself.

바쁜 식당 가면 불친절해요.
"If you go to a busy restaurant, people are not kind."
= 사람 많은 식당 가면 불친절해요.
"If you go to a restaurant with a lot of people, they're not kind."

CHAPTER 100

Saying That's Too Bad

⊗ THE WRONG WAY

다쳐서 올림픽에 못 나간다니
아쉽네요.

"It's too bad he can't go to the Olympics because he got injured."

⊘ THE RIGHT WAY

다쳐서 올림픽에 못 나간다니
안타깝네요.

"It's too bad he can't go to the Olympics because he got injured."

WHY IS THIS WRONG?

아쉽다 can translate as "to be too bad," but when you feel bad that something bad has happened to someone else, use 안타깝다 instead of 아쉽다.

NEVER MAKE THIS MISTAKE AGAIN

아쉽다 and 안타깝다 both can translate naturally as "to be too bad" — as in the expression "That's too bad." — but each verb has a different nuance:

아쉽다 This verb can be used when something feels unsatisfying — perhaps there's something missing or lacking, and you're frustrated by that. For example, you might feel 아쉽다 when you have to submit an assignment that you could have done better on if you had more time.

시간이 더 있으면 더 잘할 수 있는데... 아쉬워요.
"I could have done better if I had more time. It's too bad."

안타깝다 This verb can be used when you feel sad (or pitiful) about something. Therefore, you could use this verb when you feel sad about hearing that something unfortunate happened to someone. However, when something bad has happened to yourself, it is more natural to use 아쉽다 than 안타깝다.

제가 도와드릴 수 없어서 안타깝네요.

"I feel so sad (and frustrated) that I cannot help you."

Unnatural	Natural	Meaning
주연 씨랑 같이 못 가서 안타까워요.	주연 씨랑 같이 못 가서 아쉬워요.	"It's too bad that I can't go with Jooyeon."
석진 씨가 슬퍼한다는 얘기를 들으니 아쉽네요.	석진 씨가 슬퍼한다는 얘기를 들으니 안타깝네요.	"I feel sad to hear that Seokjin is sad."
그렇게 맛있는 것을 안 먹어 봤다니 아쉽네요.	그렇게 맛있는 것을 안 먹어 봤다니 안타깝네요.	"I feel sad that you haven't tried such a tasty thing."

MP3 audio files can be downloaded at
https://talktomeinkorean.com/audio.